Contents

Foreword   ix
   Gloria Ladson-Billings

Acknowledgments   xv

Introduction   1
   Jonathan G. Silin and Carol Lippman

PART I.   WHERE WE COME FROM   9

   1. The Newark I Knew   13
       Lillian Burke

   2. Precedents and Precautions   21
       Edna K. Shapiro

   3. Interview with Catherine M. McFarland,
       Executive Officer, The Victoria Foundation   33
       Interview by Carol Lippman

   4. Newark in Context   41
       Jonathan G. Silin and Carol Lippman

   5. The Challenges of School Reform   54
       Beverly L. Hall

   6. Interview with Marion Bolden, District
       Superintendent, The Newark Public Schools   60
       Interview by Carol Lippman

PART II.   TEACHING AND LEARNING   67

   7. This Train Is Crossing the River   71
       Betsy Blachly and Sandra Heintz

8. Creating a Caring, Democratic Classroom
    Community for and with Young Children   82
    Nancy Balaban

9. An Oasis of Humanity in a Sea of
    Bureaucratic Chaos   91
    Joan Bojsza

10. Working Together   96
    Lenore Furman and Kathleen Hayes

11. Being Like Me:
    What Newark's School Children Say About Identity   107
    Lesley Koplow

PART III. WORKING TOGETHER   113

12. Putting a Little Bass in Your Voice   117
    Felice Wagman and Mary Reaves

13. On the Bridge That We Are Building   126
    Margot Hammond with Marva Wright Banks,
    Ethel M. Cotten, Evangeline Dent, and Mary Reaves

14. What Counts for Caring?   140
    Judith W. Lesch

15. Public-Private Partnerships   152
    Augusta Souza Kappner

16. Opening One's Heart to Love, Risk, and Change:
    One Staff Developer's Journey   160
    Eileen Wasow

Appendix: Student Outcomes on District and State
Assessments for the 1996–1997 New Beginnings
Kindergarten Cohort   169
    Rosemarie Kopacsi

References   173

About the Editors and Contributors   181

Index   187

Foreword

AS AN AFRICAN-AMERICAN YOUNGSTER growing up in 1950s and 1960s Philadelphia, I learned that the way to survive the harsh assessment of the peer group was not with brawn but with brains. Kids in my neighborhood respected the spoken word and we cultivated the African-American ritual of insult known as "playing the dozens." A good dozens player was someone who could draw word pictures, create metaphors, and tease out similes. One of the places a dozens player went for material was to the object of insult's family history and heritage. In the semi-sophisticated Philadelphia—far enough North to have shed any southern traces and large enough not to be a hick town—the worst thing you could be considered was "country." However, we saved a special set of insults for people from one place— New Jersey—a place we called "the armpit of the nation."

Of course, we did not mean all of Jersey (as we say on the East Coast) when we tried to denigrate a peer. Everyone knew that growing up in Princeton, or Hopewell, or West Windsor, or even Cherry Hill was nothing to be ashamed of. But, when we talked about being from Jersey as an insult, we were referring to one of two specific places—Camden or Newark. Camden was Philadelphia's ugly stepsister. Newark so pitiful that Lady Liberty turned her back on it. However, in the summer of 1967, Newark stopped being a joke in our community.

In July 1967, 5 days of rioting in Newark placed it firmly in the consciousness of the entire nation. Although half of the voters in Newark were African Americans, they had almost no political power. This sense of hopelessness erupted, resulting in a loss of 26 lives and almost $15 million in property damage. From that moment on the name Newark, like the name Watts, became synonymous with Black dissatisfaction and frustration. Unfortunately, the newly found respect that Newark earned in my community and other African-American communities across the nation failed to turn it into a place of Black self-sufficiency and deep pride. Instead, Newark was allowed to wither on the vine. Its neighborhoods, schools, and financial infrastructure deteriorated further. What the riots did not destroy, federal and state neglect killed.

In recent years, Newark has come to be seen as a convenient point of embarkation. No one really went *to* Newark. Instead, Newark was a place through which one traveled to get somewhere else. Passengers flying into Newark were more likely coming to New York City. Newark merely provided a cheaper and more accessible gateway. Passengers flying out of Newark also were likely to be originating from some other place. Much like for Oakland, in relation to San Francisco, for Newark, there was no there, there! However, unlike Oakland, Newark has no major league professional baseball or football team. It lacks the distinctive identity and sense of place that other municipalities and areas of the state have. It does not have Princeton's quaintness and charm. It does not have Atlantic City's glamour and titillation. It does not have the quiet splendor of the Pine Barrens. Although it is New Jersey's largest city, it remains a placeholder between New York and Philadelphia in the minds of many.

Thus I come to this volume from a particular vantage point. I have seen Newark through a prism of ridicule, respect, and, now, regeneration. This volume is about one aspect of that regeneration—the work of the teachers, administrators, teacher educators, students, and their families who participated in Project New Beginnings to restructure and reform early childhood education in the Newark Public Schools.

Why is school reform in Newark important to an audience beyond New Jersey? Who would want to know about Newark when we have so much data from Chicago, New York, Tennessee, and North Carolina? What does Newark have to offer? I want to argue that this volume on Newark's Project New Beginnings offers us a unique set of perspectives on school reform—perspectives from the ground up and a more expansive vision of success. It challenges us to move outside of the narrow strictures of teaching to the test, testing, promotion or retention, and teaching to the test all over again. It offers us an opportunity to see school reform in the context of authentic education.

After the release of the 1983 report *A Nation at Risk*, America became obsessed with the notion of school restructuring and school reform. The public wanted a more coherent and rigorous curriculum. It also wanted what was termed the "best and the brightest" to enter teaching. By the 1990s, words such as *standards*, *accountability*, and *curriculum alignment* were commonplace terms to describe schooling.

Interestingly enough, what was once an entire nation at risk became a particular segment of students who were called "at risk." To no one's surprise those students deemed at risk were poor, students of color, immigrants, and second language learners.

Throughout the 1990s the nation's schools began interpreting a vast array of curriculum standards, performance indicators, and standardized tests into what history of education scholars David Tyack and Larry Cuban (1995) call the "grammar of schooling." What the public learned from this beehive of reform, restructuring, standards activity was that rich White school districts were high performing while poor districts serving children of color were low performing. Almost every large urban district is low performing and serves mostly students of color. To those who have toiled in urban school districts for many years, this disparity was not news. The so-called achievement gap is an ever-present fact of urban schools. However, the data revealed that after years of narrowing the gap, students of color in urban schools were slipping further and further behind. What the furor over school reform highlighted was just how completely White flight, an eroded tax base, and political negligence had devastated urban schools.

The awful condition of urban schools also made the schools fertile ground for a variety of research agendas and programmatic changes. The push for accountability forced urban school administrators to look for quick fixes to bring their students up to mandated academic standards. Thus prescriptive programs in reading and mathematics found their way into many urban classrooms. In some cases, these programs added to the de-skilling (Apple, 1990) of teachers because they required teachers to follow daily scripts in their teaching. Urban school districts spend millions of dollars purchasing programs that purport to boost student performance on standardized tests. And, although there have been some modest gains in some urban districts, the achievement gap between White and African-American, Latina/o, and Native-American students persists.

Where does Newark's Project New Beginnings fit into this school reform discourse? What is happening in Newark that makes it worthy of consideration? As I read this volume, I was reminded of my own work with successful teachers of African-American students (Ladson-Billings, 1994). In that work I tried to ask a very different kind of question. Instead of accepting a notion of total school failure, I wanted to understand what happens in those classrooms where teachers were able to support high levels of performance among African-American students.

I referred to the work of these teachers as "culturally relevant pedagogy" (Ladson-Billings, 1994, 1995). Their pedagogical practices rest on three propositions: academic achievement, cultural competence, and

sociopolitical consciousness. Academic achievement refers to the proficiency students are able to demonstrate as a result of pedagogical
experiences that their teachers plan and implement. Such academic
achievement is not merely student performance on standardized tests
but rather a more robust and authentic learning that students are able
to put to use in a variety of settings. Several of the chapters in this volume (e.g., chaps. 7 and 10) are excellent examples of what is meant by
academic achievement.

The second proposition, cultural competence, often is more difficult to grasp. It refers to the development of relevant cultural skills in
one's culture of origin along with that of the dominant society. Children of color and children who are English language learners must have
the opportunity to learn the dominant discourse—not to assimilate and
lose their sense of self but to participate in the civic and economic culture of their world. But they also need to be fully conversant in the
strength, beauty, and power of their own cultures. The task of teaching
in such communities is to help students become bicultural and fluent
across cultures. In several of the articles in this volume (e.g., chaps. 11,
12, 13, and 14) you will find examples of people willing to do the hard
work of culture learning. In my own teaching I have found that one of
the more difficult tasks is helping my White students understand that
they have a culture that shapes their thinking and perspectives. Once
they begin to recognize the power of culture on their own thinking, they
become more open to the idea that students' cultures help them make
sense of the world. Another point of helping teachers discover the influence of their own culture is to allay their fears about trying to learn
every student culture with which they interact. Instead, we want
teachers to recognize culture, writ large, as a learning influence as
powerful as psychological and sociological factors.

Finally, culturally relevant teaching is characterized by its attention to sociopolitical consciousness. It is not enough for students to
demonstrate academic achievement and cultural knowledge. They also
need to understand the wider social context to make sense of social
inequity and injustice. This is the kind of education Brazilian educator
Paulo Freire refers to as he sought to politicize the masses in Brazil (and
later Guinea Bissau) through literacy. The teachers in my study found
ways to engage their students in meaningful social/political activities
outside of the classroom. One teacher helped her students appeal to their
local city council concerning a vacant strip mall. Another teacher got
her students involved in a project with veterans at the local VA Hospital. In both instances, the students learned that their communities
lacked some basic goods and services and that their education could be

put to use to address those needs. In this volume, Chapters 8, 9, and 10 provide examples of how teachers can reach out beyond the traditional curriculum into the community to engage students in meaningful and powerful learning.

The real message of *Putting the Children First* is that school reform is not a generic task any more than child rearing is a generic task. Every circumstance, every setting has its own needs and challenges. School reform works when it is tailored to the specific schools and involves the active participation of the teachers, administrators, students, and families in those schools. Rather than focusing on the "things" of school reform (curriculum, tests, scheduling, organization), *Putting the Children First* focuses on the people. By highlighting the human capacity, this project was able to bring the students' success, not "school accountability," to the forefront. This volume takes the reader on a journey of hope within reform. It reminds us of the vital need for coalition and collaboration. Like the civil rights movement of the 1960s, Project New Beginnings demonstrates that success in a struggle is not about either vanguard leadership or grass-roots organizing—it is about both. This is a story not of prescription but of possibility, not of directives but of direction, not of selling out but of buying in. It is urban education at its best and the redefinition of what it means to "be from Newark."

Gloria Ladson-Billings

Acknowledgments

THE CHALLENGING WORK of school reform documented in these pages could not have proceeded without the generous support of many foundations. Although the Victoria Foundation and the Prudential Foundation took the lead during the first year, they were subsequently joined by others including the following: Allen and Joan Bildner & The Bildner Family Foundation; The Schumann Fund for New Jersey; The Healthcare Foundation of New Jersey; The Michael F. Price Foundation; the Geraldine R. Dodge Foundation; Lucent Technologies; the Charles Hayden Foundation; and the Edward M. Fitzgerald Fund at the University of Medicine and Dentistry of New Jersey. A minigrant from the Division of Continuing Education at Bank Street College supported our work on *Putting the Children First*.

The skillful guidance of Fern Khan, dean of continuing education at Bank Street College, and Gussie Kappner, its president, was critical to the success of the Newark–Bank Street collaboration. The staff members of Project New Beginnings—patient, insightful, and always ready—have our unbounded admiration as well. Across the river, the steady leadership of Marion Bolden, superintendent, and Anzella Nelms, deputy superintendent, made possible an environment in which teachers and staff developers could work together to change classroom practices.

Like many traditional foods, this book has taken a long time to prepare. Sometimes we have watched it simmer slowly and at other times we have had to adjust the ingredients to balance the flavors. Always, we have benefited from the comments of colleagues and friends who have helped us to move beyond the basic recipe with which we started. We are especially indebted to the kind and able assistance of the entire staff at Teachers College Press.

Carol Lippman thanks Jonathan Silin for his creative and respectful collaboration. Without him this book would not have seen the light

xv

of day. She is grateful too for the intellectual and emotional sustenance provided by Adrianne Kamsler and Jody Messler Davies and for the love of her family—Amy, Matthew, Rebecca, and Gary—whose faith and support have sustained her throughout.

Jonathan Silin thanks Carol Lippman for her unshakable commitment to this project, Fran Schwartz for being smart about kids and teachers, and Bob Giard for staying calm when the pot boils over.

Without the sure hands of Kristy Raska on the keyboard, this book would still be a glimmer in the chefs' eyes.

Introduction

JONATHAN G. SILIN AND CAROL LIPPMAN

FOR THE LONGEST TIME neither of us wanted to write about our work in Newark. Carol, director of Project New Beginnings, a collaboration between the Newark Public Schools and Bank Street College of Education to restructure early childhood education in that city, was immersed in the day-to-day challenges of building trust between two very different institutions. The former, a large, mostly African-American and Latino district with a traditional approach to curriculum and teaching, and the latter, a small, private, middle-class and predominately White institution with an abiding commitment to progressive practices, made an unlikely coupling. Her weekly calendar was filled to overflowing with meetings about budgets and funding, conferences with staff who excelled at their jobs and staff who needed additional supports, and visits to schools whose principals either had made deep commitments to a new way of thinking about classrooms or were more hesitant in their embrace of progressive pedagogy. There was little time to contemplate or manage the record we might leave for future school change agents.

Jonathan, in his capacity as codirector of research, was convinced that the story of school reform in poor, urban school districts had been told before in both passionately moving and coolly analytic tomes. Struggles for power and control, the duplication of programs, and the long-term impact of economic decline and racism have been described regularly, sometimes it seems almost too regularly, by scholars and journalists in academic journals and the daily press. What more could be said? What more could be done?

In truth, despite our experiences in other urban schools, we were both distressed, sometimes depressed, by what we found in Newark during the fall of 1995, just after the New Jersey Supreme Court mandated a state takeover of the district. Yes, we met many dedicated and highly skilled teachers and administrators. Yes, we explored working-class neighborhoods filled with neatly tended one- and two-family homes as well as thriving shops and small businesses. At the same time we saw too many demoralized teachers overloaded with administrative details, tugged apart by contradictory directives from the central office, and burdened with children needing counseling, social services, and medical attention. As progressive educators, we were particularly outraged to observe young children sitting quietly in their seats for most of the day while they moved together lockstep through a preset curriculum and to learn that kindergartners were required to take a 40-page written test at the end of their first year in school. We were disheartened to see teachers asked to write their goals for the day on the chalkboard each morning, so that if an administrator wandered into the classroom she or he could quickly judge if the lesson objectives were being met. Like the authors of the final report that prompted the state takeover of the district, we also observed school buildings in disrepair, the absence of sufficient, appropriate instructional materials, equipment, and supplies in classrooms, and a lack of parent involvement (Community Training and Assistance Center, 2000).

With much to do and to learn at the outset of the project, we found it all too easy to lose sight of the fact that we had become part of a unique moment in the history of education. Soon enough, however, Carol would be summoned to the state capital for a meeting with the commissioner of education about the introduction of Comprehensive School Reform (CSR) in Newark. In 1998 New Jersey became the first state in the nation to mandate the adoption of this newly popular approach to reform by all 30 of its resource-poor and low-performing districts. Later, Jonathan would hear principals and vice-principals describe the three on-site assessments of their work conducted by educational consultants, a requirement of the state takeover that led to 37 vacancies by spring 1996. Outsiders, we were brought up short by moments such as these, reminded that the Newark Public Schools are at the nexus of a series of events—state takeovers of failing districts, mandated comprehensive school reform, high-stakes testing, and public demands for accountability—that make them a symbol of all that has gone wrong in urban education and a focus of hope for those who believe in the remedies currently at hand.

New Beginnings has been far from the deus ex machina that professionals and community members might have hoped would rescue their failing system. Indeed, it has made almost every mistake that a school change project can make. This fact alone might have initially served to inhibit our writing as surely as it propelled us forward once we had started. Acquiescing to the district's initial demand, the project began with one teacher in each of 16 schools, evenly divided among Newark's four School Leadership Teams, and in the second year compounded this fragmentation by spreading to 55 classrooms in 19 schools. This structure continued to leave individual teachers isolated and the project with little ability to affect the cultures of the schools. Further, the New Beginnings presence was dictated top-down by the district with no time permitted to secure the buy-in of diverse constituencies, let alone the involvement in agenda setting, that is considered essential for successful change. Failing to secure district commitment to release time for teachers to attend workshops and regular meetings during the school day, staff developers were confined to classroom visits and required to find talk time in the margins of teachers' already busy professional lives. At the start too, an absence of clearly defined goals and objectives left many individuals without a sense of achievement and the project without benchmarks by which to measure its own successes and failures.

Despite its many deficiencies and the challenges posed by collaborating with other curricular initiatives and CSR models, New Beginnings has flourished. It has affected the lives of hundreds of teachers and administrators, thousands of students and their families. Along with new teaching strategies and improved test scores, the project has brought a better quality of life for children and adults in many schools. This is not to proclaim an answer for what ails urban education in America or even a method that might be replicated in other troubled districts but rather to affirm that over time, with persistence and flexibility, individuals and institutions can build the trusting relationships that are the foundation upon which lasting reforms are constructed.

Slowly we began to appreciate the small changes that indicate deeper shifts in teaching and learning—a teacher who had long ago consigned a dollhouse to the top shelf of her closet brings it down for her 5-year-olds to use during work period; a teacher who had never left the school building with her first graders for fear of community violence begins to take short trips to the local bodega to buy ingredients for a bread-making project; and a second-grade teacher returns to the pleasure of reading chapter books to her children during an after-lunch quiet time. Such simple but extraordinarily difficult changes are made more easily with administrative support. Increasingly calling for a tone of decency in their schools, principals were becoming educational leaders—making frequent visits to the pre-K classroom to check on the eggs hatching in a carefully tended incubator, enjoying the pizza made in the first grade as part of their study of local restaurants, and listening attentively as second graders read their stories aloud.

With growing determination we wanted to recount what was happening in New Beginnings classrooms and schools. More than that, we wanted to provide a vehicle through which others could speak the truth of school reform to the powers that control the rules and purse strings of education. We began to envision a book in which the many people involved in turning the schools around—from paraprofessionals, teachers, principals, and staff developers to school superintendents and foundation heads—could report from the front lines. This is to acknowledge that effective change is a bottom-up/top-down process and occurs in the central office as well as individual classrooms, in foundation conference rooms as well as in university think tanks. We decided to risk the coherence and seamlessness that comes with a single narrative voice in the hopes of communicating the complexity and human struggles involved in school reform.

Having extensive histories in progressive institutions, we believe that the primary issue in Newark is one of equity and social justice, not the implementation of a specific pedagogy or set of reforms. At the end of a long day, however, it is also easy to forget that a tone of decency and respect in classrooms is far more important and achievable than a particular approach to reading or math; a growing sense of collegiality among the adults who work in a given building far outweighs the implementation of a new social studies or science curriculum. The literature of school reform underlines the importance of establishing strong professional communities among teachers so as to minimize isolation and maximize opportunities for group conversation (Fullan, 1998). Communities cannot be legislated into existence. They take time to build, time in which people can establish a sense of shared purposes and a common fund of knowledge about how to achieve them. McLauglin (1998) comments:

> If teachers are not learning together, reflecting together, examining student work together, changes in governance structures, and increased site-level professional autonomy, likely will mean little in terms of student outcomes. What is most important to restructure, our research suggests, are the relationships among teachers and the organizational conditions that support discourse and strong community. (p. 81)

Education reform is seldom about either/or situations. Most often, implementing change is a matter of limited resources and power within the school system. This is to say that 6 years in the Newark Public Schools has confirmed our understanding that at heart education is a political process. Political in the most obvious sense that what happens in classrooms ultimately reflects policy decisions made in local, state, and federal legislative forums. Political too in that most schools replicate the ways that race, gender, and class are organized in the larger society. Finally, political in that educational outcomes reflect the ways that power is negotiated among people within individual classrooms and schools.

Over the last decade the volume of educational rhetoric has grown shrill with demands for standards, accountability, and privatization of public responsibilities (Clarke & Wasley, 1999). This clamor has often drowned out the voices of researchers who document the shortcomings of the high-stakes testing movement (Cuffaro, 2000; Meier, 2000). Beyond undervaluing teachers' knowledge of their students and assuming cultural homogeneity, there is evidence that standards-based instruction narrows the curriculum, increases grade-level retention, negatively affects graduation rates for minority students, and does not improve future economic performance (Levin, 1998; Linn, 2000). Also lost in the din are the voices of those who remind us that education is an ethical and moral, as well as political, process (Greene, 1995). For embedded in the daily practices of teachers and administrators are different conceptions of the good life and the just society. Politicians, with their eyes on the future, tend to want schools to turn out more highly skilled workers or better scientists and divert attention from the present, from the quality of life in the here and now. The authors in this volume confirm our commitment to viewing education as an ethical practice, one that shapes how people interact with and care for one another from minute to minute and hour to hour.

Many books about urban school reform have preceded this one and many will follow it. Some (Kozol, 1992) are of the muck-raking variety in the tradition of Jacob Riis and Joseph Meyer Rice. They arm us with facts and heartbreaking stories of the dispossessed as we pursue our work on behalf of a better society. Others (Kohl, 1967; Meier, 1995), in the *Stand and Deliver* tradition, tell how hard-working, driven, often charismatic teachers have transformed individual classrooms and entire schools. They remind us that dedication can overcome adversity and that change occurs one classroom and one school at a time. Yet others (Tyack & Cuban, 1995) offer more scholarly accounts of the big picture, of how currents of reform ebb and flow as part of the larger sociopolitical contexts of which schools are a part. We are inspired too by the authors (Aronowitz & Giroux, 1991; Freire, 1986) who prod us to imagine new worlds and the radical forms of education that can help us to achieve them. We are indebted as well to the authors (Delpit, 1995; Fine, Weis, Powell, & Wong, 1997; Ladson-Billings, 1994) who teach us about the never-to-be-forgotten complexities of race and class as they are played out in American schools.

It would be disingenuous to suggest that we haven't tried to shape our own volume by identifying voices that we thought should be heard. At moments this has meant pushing first-time authors to put their thoughts into words, convincing them that they indeed have a story that would interest others. It has also meant going out with tape recorder and notebook to talk with busy administrators who could not find the time to set pen to paper. Unexpectedly, teachers who had taught writing process to young children and were comfortable asking their students for multiple drafts of stories and reports now faced the return of their own second and third drafts with requests for more detail and less generalization, more action and less description. We empathized with our authors and tried to honor their intent and voice, even as we demanded that they craft essays that would engage the reader, essays that were by turn evocative and analytic, descriptive and critical. We believe that everyone has been successful in her own way. And together these essays make a richly textured, whole cloth with far more depth and many more dimensions than any single author could have achieved. Most important, educators in Newark and New York have spoken for themselves about what it means to cross the river in order to learn from each other.

Putting the Children First is divided into three parts, each containing chapters written by Newark Public School personnel or Bank Street staff developers or both together. The essays in Part I, Where We Come From, lay the foundation for understanding the challenge of collaboration between two very different partners. The history of Newark and its schools as well as Bank Street's involvement in public education are explored. At the center of the book, Part II, Teaching and Learning, depicts some of the changes that have occurred in Newark classrooms as teachers and staff developers share common passions. Here is ample evidence that effective curriculum, curriculum that matters to children, must be grounded in teachers' commitment to the world of which they are a part, no matter its shortcomings and inequities. In Part III, Working Together, the essays attend directly to the business of bridging the distances between individuals and cultures. A central concern for many of these authors is the question of race and its intersections with class and gender. They demonstrate that successful partnerships require the articulation of difference and, as often as not, greater changes in the agent of change than in those she or he seeks to influence.

Although we have tried to organize the essays thematically, inevitably life overflows the simplified categories we construct to contain it. Essays on history are filled with discussions about curriculum, essays on curriculum development cannot bypass the interpersonal dynamics of change, and essays about the change process inevitably circle back to take up curricular matters. It is this very multilayered quality of the essays that makes them real and provocative, redolent with the past and hopeful about the future.

Finally, these essays and, more important, the changes that have occurred in New Beginnings schools—children moving calmly, purposefully, and independently in classrooms that offer choices of activities and materials—speak as much to issues of social justice as they do to strategies for restructuring school governance, as much about values that respect the student as actor attempting to make meaning of her experience as they do to the details of school budgets and demands of state standards. In saying this, we do not mean to give short shrift to the dailiness of life in schools but rather to suggest that meaningful reform must be powered by social purposes that may be embedded in many different kinds of programs. As educators, we have learned anew to value the small but important shifts in the ways that teachers talk to children, parents, and colleagues, the sense of community that they foster in their classrooms, and their willingness to take risks in the interests of creating more socially relevant curriculum. And for our part, we have learned to honor the knowledge and values of those whom we would purport to change, to recognize how easy it is to become stuck in the familiar and well rehearsed, and to respect the time it takes to get from one place to another, especially when the place from which we have started and the place at which we hope to arrive keep slipping from view.

PART I

WHERE WE COME FROM

PROJECT NEW BEGINNINGS began under less than ideal circumstances—in the wake of a state takeover, the stepchild of a new, court-appointed superintendent, and without adequate time to secure buy-in from teachers or schools. Despite these constraints, many Bank Street staff developers and Newark teachers managed to establish what might conservatively be characterized as a tentative trust during the first years. Often coming from very different backgrounds and holding very different educational commitments, the participants worked hard to negotiate a shared agenda, to locate common ground. Beyond the rhetoric of reform and the talk about the best interests of the children, how would daily classroom practices change? How would teachers balance the ongoing requirements of the district with the new ideas being offered by the project?

From the start the look of New Beginnings classrooms was radically transformed by the arrival of truckloads of furniture and curriculum materials purchased with generous foundation support. Classrooms were abloom with sand and water tables, art materials, blocks, and math manipulatives. The many new interest centers prompted teachers to give children more choices and responsibility for their own learning than in the past. Teachers in turn began to work with individuals and small groups rather than the entire class and to focus on building community in the classroom. When a conflict about space broke out in the block area, a group meeting was called so that the children themselves could arrive at a solution and, when a child came to school preoccupied with family events—the birth of a baby sister, the incarceration of a revered uncle, or the death of a favorite grandmother—time was made so that teachers and peers could listen to the story and render support. Adjusting to noisy, busy environments with multiple activities and flexible scheduling was harder for some teachers and administrators than for others. And, despite the fact that after the first year New Beginnings students had the highest scores on the dreaded year-end kindergarten test (Kopacsi & Hochwald, 1997), concerns about how they would fare on future standardized tests abounded (see Appendix).

Along with a more child-centered, activity-based curriculum, New Beginnings brought with it a series of dilemmas for teachers and staff developers. For their part, teachers were pleased with the new freedoms and responsibilities accorded them in New Beginnings classrooms (Schwartz & Silin, 1998). Most important, with the time and opportunity to observe children more closely, they could make curriculum decisions that were "developmentally appropriate." Teachers were deeply disappointed, however, in the project's inability to ameliorate District/School Leadership Team practices with which they disagreed, such as extensive testing, traditional lesson plans, the use of basal readers, and the influx of curriculum initiatives that drew them away from hands-on activities with children. The majority of teachers felt themselves torn between "two masters" who often asked them to teach in completely different ways. After the first year of the project, a kindergarten teacher commented:

> I felt caught all the time. It was like I had to play a game . . . I was saying to myself I want to do this Bank Street thing deep in my heart. But I'm the only Bank Street teacher. At grade level meetings I understood that what was said for others was also expected of me. The administrator required that every teacher give the same tests, every week.

Caught between two approaches to education, some teachers tried to "hedge their bets," adopting just enough from New Beginnings to appear permeable to its influence while maintaining sufficient practices from the past to be confident that their students would meet district-wide standards. Others, devoted the mornings to traditional practices and "did Bank Street" in the afternoon, whereas still others, more committed to a child-centered philosophy, found ways of meeting district goals by more fully employing New Beginnings practices.

For their part, staff developers often reported being taken aback by the deep poverty of some communities and the harsh environments they found in many schools. The absence of clearly articulated New Beginnings goals as well as the commitment to an evolving curriculum, combined with their own reluctance to impose on teachers and the absence of a strong mandate from building-level administrators, contributed to tensions between staff developers and teachers. Even as there were differences in expectations, staff devel-

opers received greatest satisfaction from working with individual
teachers. A staff developer comments:

> What we are saying is that Bank Street is about making a rela-
> tionship. I think the relationship part of teaching and good
> educational practice is one of the things that brings us all to this
> table. . . . Part of what happens in the beginning is that I come
> into a classroom, the teacher hasn't asked for me . . . and she has
> been doing her number with her kindergarten kids and so she
> asks: What's the Bank Street way? What's the program now?
>
> I don't have a bag of tricks to hand her. I do have myself and
> my experience and knowledge of teaching. But that doesn't come
> in a Bank Street handbook. I think we all struggled with that as
> we walked into classrooms with teachers who have been as-
> saulted by other programs to make them better.
>
> It's not pushing Bank Street away but it's struggling with a
> kind of request, a need for internal and external structure. And
> something to offer that is both more and less than a guidebook.

Daily, staff developers experienced a set of ethical dilemmas
stemming from their strong commitment to honor the values, knowledge, and experiences of the families and teachers of Newark while
realizing their roles as change agents. Drawing on Richardson's (1992)
description of this *agenda-setting dilemma*, Putnam and Borko (2000)
comment:

> The staff developer wants to see teachers' practice change in particular
> directions while empowering the teachers themselves to be meaning-
> fully involved in determining the changes. This dilemma is analogous
> to one faced by the classroom teacher who wants to empower children
> to build upon their own thinking while simultaneously ensuring that
> they learn expected subject-matter content. Staff developers, like
> teachers, must negotiate their way between the learners' current
> thinking and the subject matter or content to be learned. In the case of
> staff development, the "learners" are teachers and the "content" is
> typically new teaching practices and forms of pedagogical thinking. (p. 9)

In the early years, staff developers vacillated between hopeful-
ness about the outcomes of their work and despair about their ability
to offset the entrenched impact of poverty and racism. Along with
teachers, staff developers struggled with how to respond to the
realities of poor housing, inadequate health care and nutrition, and
community violence, within the parameters of their professional

lives. Most chose to focus on the tasks of fostering more humane and child-friendly environments in the school and helping to link the schools with community providers of health and social services. Staff developers struggled with the added paradox of being change agents employed by mainstream institutions, complicit in a system of private foundations that would soon enough withdraw support and move on to other programs, in different cities.

The essays in Part I, Where We Come From, offer insight into both the history of Newark and its public schools and the traditions with which Bank Street staff developers arrived on the scene. Three chapters are written by people who grew up in and around Newark and who went on to spend their professional lives either in the Newark Public Schools or closely affiliated with them. Lillian Burke describes a 1950s Newark childhood, coming to teach in the schools a decade later amidst the social upheaval of the 1960s, and her current work as a principal. Marion Bolden, also a product of Newark's public schools, describes a different Newark childhood and, as the current superintendent, outlines a vision for the future of the district. Cathy McFarland offers a perspective on the summer riots of 1967, events that led to her participation in the schools as a parent, volunteer, and ultimately executive officer of the Victoria Foundation, the first and most consistent funder of the Newark–Bank Street collaboration. Beverly Hall, the first court-appointed state district superintendent of the Newark Public Schools, recounts the difficult early days of the state takeover. Two additional essays in Part I are authored by Bank Streeters. Edna Shapiro tracks the history of the college's involvement in public education; and we (Silin and Lippman) look at the social and political contexts shaping reform efforts in Newark. Together, these essays lay the foundation for understanding the challenges of collaboration and the classroom achievements documented in Part II.

1

The Newark I Knew

LILLIAN BURKE

Lillian Burke has been the principal of Clinton Avenue Elementary School since New Beginnings began in September 1996. At that time, there was just one New Beginnings kindergarten class in her school. She became committed to the project when, along with the first cohort of teachers and administrators, she traveled to Pittsburgh to visit Bank Street's Vision 21 schools. She came back determined to make all the classrooms in her school reflect developmentally appropriate practices. In the second year of the project, Clinton Avenue was designated a pilot school. New Beginnings expanded into all five kindergartens and first grades with the goal of reaching the second and third grades in the following year. With the support of Burke, the school has continued to be a site at which the project has experimented with many of its new initiatives. Sitting in the school library on a crisp fall day, she told her story to Carol Lippman in the clear, thoughtfully composed sentences that characterize her speech.

I WAS BORN AT BARNABAS HOSPITAL on High Street in Newark. I attended elementary school in that city and am a graduate of West Side High School. With the exception of the 3 years that I spent as a military wife in Texas and Madrid, I have lived my entire life in either Newark or East Orange. I continue to live in Newark today.

The city has undergone enormous changes since I was a child and not just in the area of education; the entire city is different. Most people

who come from Newark are ambivalent about it. They recollect all those
things that made them love the city and, at the same time, hate what
the city has become.

Growing up in Newark during the 1950s was a very rich experience.
There were always events happening. The school system sponsored an
extensive after-school program where I learned tennis, roller skating,
and board games of all kinds. During the summer there were playground
programs and I participated in square dancing, folk dancing, and cooking activities. There were always Girl Scout and Boy Scout programs,
football and baseball leagues, as well as a city chorus and orchestra.
There were even academic scholarships for exceptional children.

My sister had been a member of a theatrical group that worked with
WBGO, the radio station at Central High School. She would leave school
2 or 3 days a week and go to the station, where she would be part of a
radio play. I can remember that in third grade we studied the Indians
who originally inhabited this area, the Lenne Lanape. WBGO would
regularly present a short drama about an Indian boy or girl and we would
hear the voices of actual Newark students coming over the school radio
station. That is an experience I will never forget.

We had a very fine educational system at that time, and as children we were told that other school districts around the country visited Newark to see our practices. One of the first principals' associations
was founded here and is still in existence. The Newark Teachers' Association also gave birth to New Jersey's Education Association. We
were in the vanguard, at the forefront of good education.

I attended Newark State College, which is only a few miles outside of the city in Union, New Jersey. I was recruited by the City of
Newark for my junior practicum and my senior year of student teaching so that I would have a sense of teaching in an urban environment.
Along with most of my friends, I signed a contract with the Newark
Public Schools before I graduated. We were encouraged to believe that
we were joining an elite group of teachers. For example, you had to take
the national teacher's exam and at that time it wasn't required in many
other districts. We also had to be interviewed by a panel of educators
before we were offered a position.

OUTRAGED BY INJUSTICE

In 1967, the year of the riots, I was in my first year of teaching. Although
the riots were sparked by an incident between an African-American man
and the police, the city was probably feeling what the rest of nation was

feeling. There was unrest all over the country; remember it was the '60s. That summer there was a Black Power conference in the city. People traveled from across the country, from Los Angeles and Detroit, to attend the conference. It was interesting and inspiring, and in many ways very uplifting. Not the kind of event you would think would cause a riot. But the people, the mayor and others in city government, were sensitized to what was happening to the citizens of Newark. They were outraged by the injustices we had to endure. People were ready to stand up and speak out and say that they wouldn't tolerate it anymore.

The riots were ugly. But it was also frightening to see the way that the people were treated by the National Guard. The city became a police state. Not everyone participated in the riots. But everyone became subject to stops by the police. If you worked outside of Newark and you tried to return, you had to show an ID to prove that you lived in the city.

The National Guard, we called them "weekend warriors," are not full-time military and they were obviously scared to death. Unfortunately, they had guns in their hands and they were walking the streets. We were as afraid of them as they were of us because they were unpredictable and frightened. If you made what seemed to be a wrong or threatening move, they would respond very differently than trained police officers. So for the most part people tended to stay in their homes. There was a curfew too.

I worked with the Freedom Party, a third party led by George Richardson, a former Newark assemblyman. He had an office on Clinton Avenue. It was difficult to get food in the larger stores because trucks either couldn't or wouldn't enter the city to make deliveries. A lot of the smaller candy stores and mom-and-pop places where people used to get their cigarettes and provisions like milk, bread, and fresh produce were not getting supplies either. This went on for at least a week. I was part of a crew of volunteers who distributed bags of food to the community around Clinton Avenue. These provisions came from George Richardson's office. He had been able to release some trucks to enter the city.

Newark in those days was as close to a war zone as I've ever seen. The city still has the scars, 30 years later. There are areas that have never been redeveloped. Some people, out of frustration, because of how they had been treated by landlords, destroyed the houses in which they lived. If you ride around Newark today, you can still see many vacant lots. They are the result of the buildings that were burned and never replaced. In subsequent years the projects were torn down too. They are just rebuilding many of them now, but not with enough units for all those who were displaced during the riots.

The Central Ward was where most of the activity occurred, but it had a ripple effect throughout the city. For example, people in the South Ward fled. It still has all these beautiful, large, one-family homes that were once occupied by upper-middle-class Americans who finally decided that they could not stay in Newark. Some businesses left too, which meant job shortages. The riots led to the total devastation of the city.

There were dramatic changes in the schools after 1967. The problems of recruitment and retention of teachers were intensified because a lot of people were frightened and deserted the district. A real attempt was made, however, to include more African Americans in administrative and teaching positions. As part of this effort some of the standards for entry-level teachers were eliminated. First they abolished the panel interview and then the national teacher's examination requirements were lowered. In the end, the new teachers coming into Newark didn't go through the same screening process as I had and the schools were allowed to erode even further. I don't think the state did much to monitor the educational system for at least 10 years after the riots.

TWO NEIGHBORHOODS, TWO SCHOOLS

After working in a number of teaching positions in the district, I was offered a position as a vice-principal in the South Ward, at Bragaw Avenue School. In making the decision to accept that position, I followed the same path that I've been on from the time I graduated from college. If there was a service that needed to be rendered, I assumed that I was probably more adept at rendering it than someone who wasn't as familiar with the community as I was. Transferring to Bragaw Avenue School was what I was supposed to do, and I had a good experience there.

After Bragaw, I was offered the principalship at Clinton Avenue School. Making that move required a huge leap of faith. Bragaw was and still is a community school in which families know each other. Many of the parents have attended the school themselves. The neighborhood is a little alcove cut off by Route 78. Families have lived there for two and three generations, and teachers know the mothers and grandmothers of the children they teach. Bragaw is a larger facility than Clinton, but smaller because of its feeling of community. Clinton Avenue School, on a major street in the midst of Newark, has a very different feeling. All of the activity that could possibly happen on a busy street in this urban environment happens here. There are drug deals, stolen cars, and police all within the blocks immediately surrounding the school. The area doesn't have the sense of community that I felt at Bragaw just a few streets away.

At Clinton I found an experienced staff that had been part of a regimented, tightly controlled system. Children walked down the hall in straight lines. They were very good at entering and exiting the bathroom. It was all very orderly. I sat back and observed in those first months. I didn't change a lot of things.

I was eager to see if I could find some way to alter that culture. I wanted to give teachers a sense of ownership, of instructional responsibility. I'll give you an example. The students had always received basal readers along with accompanying workbooks. Soon after I arrived, a first-grade teacher approached me and asked if the children would be allowed to write in the workbooks. I immediately wanted to know if this was a trick question. I said, "They are first graders," and she said, "Yes, but they haven't been allowed to write in the workbooks." They had to write on a separate piece of paper. I told her, "No, they are going to write in the workbooks from now on." She asked, "But what if next year we don't have enough money for workbooks?" And I replied, "well then we'll think of something else. This year they are going to write in the workbooks."

At Clinton Avenue School I immediately noticed that the teachers were very focused on decorating the walls to compensate for the fact that there were no windows in the school. The building was constructed in 1969, right after the riots, to alleviate overcrowding at Brown Academy. I don't know whose idea it was to build a cinder-block building with no windows for primary children, and no real play area either, but that was what was done! It was a kind of architectural statement about trying to keep the confusion of what's on the outside from being noticed by the children on the inside. As if that were possible! The children bring it all in their heads and in their conversations; and most importantly they live it. You can't make a school a closed environment.

There are families coming and going all the time in the Clinton Avenue area. There are lots of transients here causing a high mobility rate. In the Bragaw community, only a few blocks away, there are one- or two-family homes frequently occupied by the owners, their children, and grandchildren. There is a much more stable population.

There are churches near the school—a large number, perhaps five or six—but the people who attend them don't live in this community any longer. For the most part, people don't walk to church, they drive. Some of those churchgoers have left Newark. Some live in other sections of the city or farther into the South toward Hillside.

In order to really understand the Clinton community, you have to observe the folks walk up and down the street and go in and out of the stores or watch them on Saturday as I sometimes do. They kind of know each other. There is a history in this school too. There are some staff who attended the school and sent their children here as well. So there is some sense of community, but not as tight as in other sections of Newark. The Clinton Hill section of the South Ward has become a neighborhood of lower income people and absentee landlords. This doesn't lend itself to the building of community spirit. We are two or three blocks from the heart of the Central Ward, which has the lowest income level in Newark.

A NEWARK CHILDHOOD

Since the riots, this neighborhood has been primarily African-American. It isn't the only African-American community in Newark. I know—my parents grew up in Newark. My mother attended West Side High School. I have two, going on three, generations of family in Newark. Before the 1950s African Americans lived in various parts of the city. But during the great migration of the 1950s when Blacks left the South and came North, they were herded into a few sections of the city. Here, people without enough money to buy their own homes had to rent from absentee landlords. The deterioration of the city that started before the riots was created by the housing situation.

There has always been talk about how Newark residents burned down their houses to get the insurance money. People have often asked me how people could destroy their own homes. I have lived it and want to make it clear. We didn't own our houses. We owned very little. The absentee landlords did some of the destruction so that they could benefit from the insurance money. It was arson for business. And arson for business became arson for anger. Housing was bad. Jobs were nonexistent. It was not a good time. Many businesses left after the riots, but even prior to that, if you were African-American it was difficult to get a job downtown. There were many places where African Americans couldn't work. Places that you would have thought would be logical places for them to work, such as the department stores. Back then, you might see an African American running the elevator, or doing the janitorial work, but rarely did you see them in visible locations. Race, and race-based discrimination, was a major factor in the Newark unrest.

In the '50s mostly non–African Americans worked in the schools. When I was in elementary school, I had some African-American teachers but at junior high and high school there were fewer and fewer. Even in the heart of the Central Ward where I grew up, there were not many

African-American teachers. At West Side High School, there was only one African American on the staff, the music teacher. Then toward the end of the year, the principal left and the new principal was African-American. So now we had two African Americans on staff. It was a terrible message for the students. The standards were very high and we knew we were expected to do well, but we didn't have role models to follow. The few we had, I remember well.

However, in my family there was a whole different attitude about education. My brother, sister, and I were the first in the family to finish college. A lot of this had to do with my mother; she had a certain sense of expectation. She graduated from high school and was a beautician. My dad was a construction worker. Like me, my friends were also expected to finish high school, no matter how limited their parents' schooling had been. There was no question about that. Education was important. It didn't matter that some parents couldn't help you with homework; you had to do it.

We walked to the library every week. My mother was religious about that. She got all three of us buttoned up and we went to the local library. We'd get books there, and then all would walk home together. It makes a big difference. Today, children are more confined because of the lack of security in this city. Years ago my siblings and I went to the local playground every afternoon without our parents. We sold candy bars from door to door. We played outside with our friends on our block within voice distance of my mother. We learned street games—jump rope, ring-a-lievo, hopscotch—and all those social skills that go with them too. You can't do that anymore.

I had a lot of support at home, in church, and from the community. There were always many community people around encouraging us. People said, "The Walker kids are going to succeed." Today I don't feel that pressure from the Clinton community. People who might have said, "We're not going to let you stand on the corner and get in trouble. We know your parents are concerned about you. You go home," are no longer there. If I were standing on the corner with a bunch of girls, it would be nothing for Ms. Richardson or one of the women on the block to say, "Whatcha doin' girl? Why you standing there? You know your mother'll have a fit if she saw you standing here. Go home."

Most parents don't allow their children to play outside at all. They come to school, they take them home, and they lock them inside. Children watch television, they have video games, but they are lacking the freedom that we had to go outside and play. Parents are afraid of drugs, guns, and all the rest of "what goes on down the street." You buy your child a bike, you let her go outside to ride the bike, and then it is stolen.

You buy your child roller skates and someone takes them off your child's feet. If you buy a nice pair of sneakers, somebody takes them from your child. A leather jacket can get you killed. It's a whole different environment in some sections, even though it is the same city.

Now there is enormous pressure on the schools to provide what parents can't. Pressure to have longer days and more activities, and more stimulation. It is not just books and paper and structure that children need. Some of the experiences that we had growing up we have to design for our children in school. I don't think children have changed in a hundred years. They have the same need to be fed, clothed, housed, and to feel secure. And they have the same need to be introduced to things and be stimulated and guided by mature adults. Those systems are not in place in our community anymore to support the children in the inner city. In many ways, the community, parents, and staff, we have all failed our children terribly.

When I was a child, my brother and sister took piano lessons. Their teacher mandated that we go to see the New Jersey Orchestra play at Symphony Hall. I was the youngest in the family and, although I loved the music, I often fell asleep during the concerts. I was especially impressed with Symphony Hall. It was a beautiful place, and seeing an orchestra just appear out of nowhere—having had that experience and knowing that children in the city of Newark didn't have that for many years makes me very sad. Now it's heartening to have the New Jersey Performing Arts Center, to see businesses and companies coming back, and to witness the revitalization of downtown with new stores and homes. I am proud to be part of a changing school system that once again values education, respects families, and has highly qualified leadership. We still have a long way to go to become the Newark that I once knew as a child, but we are finally moving in the right direction.

2

Precedents and Precautions

Edna K. Shapiro

*Edna Shapiro is research psychologist emeritus at Bank Street College
and co-author of the 1972* Teachers College Record *article that
defined the developmental-interaction approach to early childhood
education. In this chapter she documents two of the college's major
forays into public education—Lucy Sprague Mitchell's Public School
Workshops of the 1940s and the federally funded Follow Through
program begun in the late 1960s. Shapiro describes an important
component of the history that Bank Streeters bring to their work in
Newark and the more general challenges faced by progressive educators working in public systems.*

RECURRENT PUBLIC OUTCRY about dismal conditions in
American public schools predictably leads to a plethora of uncoordinated innovative institutions and prescriptions for reform-
ing and restructuring schooling from preschool on. Each wave of reformers brings some new ideas and many that are reminiscent of earlier
efforts. Unfortunately, very few seem to be aware of what has been
learned in previous forays into the educational system.

New Beginnings' work in the Newark Public Schools follows in a
long tradition of interventions in public education at Bank Street College. In the early days of the 20th century, Lucy Sprague Mitchell initiated a small school for very young children in tandem with a research
group. The enterprise was named the Bureau of Educational Experiments, and later became the Bank Street College of Education. The
bureau was one of a number of programs that functioned on a small scale

but with large-scale ambitions. Mitchell believed that it was important to find out more about children's needs and interests and how they learned in order to devise educational environments to enhance their growth. She viewed the fledgling nursery school as a laboratory and also as a model. With other social reformers of her time she shared a powerful commitment to finding ways to make social institutions more equitable, to build a more caring and just society (see Antler, 1987). Staff at the bureau had a dual focus. They wanted not only to create a "good life for children" but also to have a salutary influence on the public schools. Education was a means for furthering social goals.

Progressive educators combined a heightened awareness of poverty and social inequity with an optimistic and sincere belief in the power of knowledge—especially scientific knowledge—to lead to a better world. The teachers at the bureau created what today we would call a network of colleagues with compatible philosophies who exchanged ideas and reported on activities and programs they had tried out in their classrooms. They wrote about the importance of recording their observations of the behavior of the children in their classrooms, using these records to advance their understanding both of the children and of their own practices; they discussed the meanings of key terms and ideas such as curriculum, exploration, and indicators of growth. One can get a sense of their dedication, enthusiasm, and the breadth of their concerns from a selection of their reports reprinted in Winsor (1973).

The climate today is more cynical, perhaps more realistic about the difficulties of creating an educational system that enables children to learn and grow in a caring and intellectually challenging environment genuinely responsive to their needs. We have learned that large-scale bureaucracies like school systems are bulwarks of resistance to change, and many individuals are at best ambivalent about new ventures. Nevertheless, there are still those who maintain the conviction that education can bring opportunity and facilitate the development of more equitable social arrangements. Over the decades Bank Street staff has participated in many programs designed to bring "newer," "more modern," more progressive, more child-friendly and teacher-friendly, and more culturally relevant ways of teaching to public schools in a variety of localities. Such efforts may be greeted with misunderstanding, indifference, or hostility. Indeed, they are subversive to the extent that they seek to destabilize the system.

In this chapter I offer thumbnail sketches of two programs that can be considered precursors of New Beginnings: The Public School Workshops in New York City schools initiated by Mitchell in the 1940s, and the federally funded Follow Through program that spanned more than two decades, beginning in the late 1960s. Although very different in scope—the number of staff and of schools involved—as well as in the social and political contexts in which they took place, both have been well documented and illustrate the kinds of successes and obstacles such endeavors are likely to encounter. Their successes and problems have their counterparts in the experiences of New Beginnings staff.

PROGRAM CHARACTERISTICS

All three programs—the Public School Workshops, Follow Through, and New Beginnings—can be considered exemplary in the sense that they meet high standards for educational interventions. A recent social policy report by Henrich, Brown and Aber (1999) discusses issues involved in evaluating the effectiveness of school-based intervention programs. Although its focus is on projects designed to minimize violence, the report synthesizes the conclusions of a wide range of intervention efforts to arrive at three general principles for assessing program design and implementation.

- Programs should evolve from a *theoretical basis*.
- They should consist of *multiple components* that facilitate both person-centered and environmental change. This means that the program should involve not only those targets for intervention, but peers, administrators, parents, all who are connected to the target population.
- They should be of *extended duration*, spanning multiple years; evaluations also should assess cumulative and long-term effects. Short-term programs tend to have only short-term effects.

These principles adduced by Henrich, Brown, and Aber are based on meta-analysis of 177 intervention programs and serve as apt descriptors of the approach to effecting change that has characterized the work of Bank Street staff. Indeed, the principles are similar to those that informed earlier Bank Street efforts to change school practice (see Feldman, Horton, & Niemeyer, 1975).

Theoretical Basis

A fundamental principle expressed in many of Mitchell's writings is that learning is vital to life. Children and adults want to learn, but learning must be connected to life experience. Neither the child nor the adult is viewed as a passive recipient of information, but as a person with feelings as well as thoughts, a social being who needs active participation in the learning process. In the 1930s and 1940s this was expressed as teaching the "whole child." Active participation includes the idea that it is necessary to find ways to represent new knowledge, to formulate or reformulate what one has taken from the experience. Teachers too need opportunities for learning experiences that stimulate their growth and development, that push them to question received ideas and to have a fuller understanding of the social forces that have shaped their own thinking (see Mitchell, 1950, 2000).

Over the years the theoretical base has been more fully explicated (see, e.g., Biber, 1984; Nager & Shapiro, 2000; Shapiro & Biber, 1972; Shapiro & Nager, 1999). We speak of the *developmental-interaction* approach rather than the Bank Street approach because the fundamental principles and practices are not limited to Bank Street but are shared with other like-minded educational institutions.

Multiple Components

Programs developed at Bank Street characteristically have many components, covering a wide range of topics including strategies for details of scheduling and room arrangement, how to plan a trip and extend the learning opportunities, how to encourage children's use of materials in creative ways, as well as more general and theoretical concerns that may require rethinking of fundamental assumptions about schooling (see, e.g., Cuffaro, Nager, & Shapiro, 2000). Topics include learning more about how children of different ages and adults learn and grow, how cultural differences affect one's view of the world and ways of processing information, and the need to make explicit the tacit implications of one's long-held views. Work in the classroom is a primary focus, but it is equally essential to be attentive to the adults in the system so as to affect processes of interaction and coordination with other teaching, support, and administrative staff, and with parents and community representatives.

Extended Duration

The goals are to create extensive shifts in teachers' and administrators' concepts and practices. It is well known that many ambitious intervention efforts have been undertaken without solid long-term financial and administrative support. Nevertheless, it must be understood that it would be foolhardy to undertake such a program without expecting a commitment of multiple years. Ideally, the commitments involve the supporters, site representatives, and the staff of the intervention program.

These criteria apply to the two programs described here—the Public School Workshops and Follow Through—and are equally descriptive of the New Beginnings program in Newark.

THE PUBLIC SCHOOL WORKSHOPS

Although the 1940s were turbulent in many ways—World War II was in process and many people's lives were in disarray—it was also a period when the public education system of New York City was engaged in self-examination and curriculum revision. Mitchell and her colleagues had long been eager to have a chance to work in the public system, and in 1943 they were given that opportunity by the board of education. The Workshop program began in an elementary school in the West Harlem neighborhood of uptown Manhattan and was then extended to two more schools, one in Washington Heights, the other in Harlem. Many members of the Bank Street staff worked in the schools. In her 1950 book, *Our Children and Our Schools*, Mitchell reports the history of the program and describes its goals and activities, with anecdotes and details of teaching strategies and curricular units that were developed over the course of the Workshop years. In addition, I have learned more facts about the program from conversations with one of the original Workshop participants (A. F. Shapiro, personal communication, February 2001).

At first there was some inevitable wariness: What was Bank Street going to get out of this? In fact, the primary reward for the Workshop staff was the satisfaction they gained from introducing the new ideas and teaching methods in which they believed so strongly into classrooms, and having the opportunity to convince the teachers to permanently adopt the more progressive approach. Mitchell and her colleagues must have been excellent saleswomen as well as inspired teachers. They presented the outline of the Workshop idea to the teachers and made clear that it would be on a voluntary basis but would require weekly meetings after school. In the first school they were gratified that 26 of 58 teachers volunteered to participate. (It should probably be noted that the principal was eager to have the Workshop program in his school, so it is likely that there was some pressure on teachers to join in.)

They were bringing the good news about modern ways of teaching. As the program continued, more teachers wanted to become members. After 3 years, the board of education assigned three teachers—graduates of the Workshop program—to become members of the Workshop staff. Thus the board made a substantial financial as well as supportive commitment to the project.

Mitchell and her Workshop staff wrote many documents for the teachers, and for each other; one staff member wrote stories for the children partly because few stories were then available "with content familiar to these children or directly related to their programs" (Mitchell, 1950, p. 355) and partly to encourage the teachers to write such stories. They developed what they called Source Material Libraries to help implement the new curriculum and worked to get student teachers (from Bank Street and New York University) placed in the public schools.

Mitchell (1950) writes:

> We believe in having educational content in the curriculum closely related to the lives and needs of the children in any school. . . . Naturally, the question often arose: Should curriculum content and experiences planned for the children in our school be influenced by the fact that so many of these children were Negroes? (p. 365)

After much discussion among themselves, staff invited a group of leaders in the Harlem community to discuss the problem with them and the school principal. The general conclusions were that:

> The part played by Negroes in the present and past development of our country should be given somewhat greater emphasis in the social studies curriculum than is usual but that such emphasis should be put in the curriculum for *all* children; that the present trends in schools to have a "unit" on Negroes or a "Negro Week" was false though well-intentioned. (p. 368)

Their thoughtful deliberations have resonance today.

The core of their approach was the use of social studies to create an integrated curriculum. Mitchell was an avid geographer (see Mitchell, 1934/1991). Her geography was not the cut and dried recitation of capitals and major products but the study of what she called "human geography" dealing with the impact of "earth forces" on human lives. This was essentially an ecological approach, long before most people had heard the term. Children and teachers made maps and dioramas of the local landscape. Most important, they took trips to see firsthand the contours of their environment and people at work. Maps also were a vital tool for extending the study of historical eras and distant cultures that were the focus of social studies in the later grades.

One can get a sense of the content and scope of the Workshops by sampling the titles of the 27 appendices, each two or three pages, in Mitchell's book. The first is How Our Workshop Functioned Within the School System; then, Brief Write-ups of Individual Children; Dramatic Play Suggestions; How to Conduct Discussions Related to the Activity; Some Techniques to Use in Taking Children on Trips; Neighborhood Study for First Grade; Suggestions for Post Office Play, Second Grade; First-Grade Charts; Workshop Meeting: Using New York as a Laboratory; Suggestions for Discussion With Children on Roads (includes railroads, water roads, airways); Workshop Meeting: Maps as Tools for Thinking; Sixth-Grade Play About "Atomic Energy" With Preliminary Notes.*

The Workshops predated contemporary efforts at independent evaluation of program. Evidence of its success is anecdotal, primarily the enthusiastic reports of participant principals and teachers. Mitchell's book documents the first 6 years of the program; Mitchell was chair for the first 3 years, followed by Charlotte B. Winsor. The program lasted into the late 1960s. The staff worked in dozens of elementary schools in Manhattan and Brooklyn; they also gave courses for credit for participating teachers. It is not known why the program was terminated; one day the board of education announced to the staff that it was finished, with no explanation. Some of the principals and teachers continued to take part in Bank Street College functions, and several of the Workshop staff continued to work with Bank Street staff in public schools in other sites. One exemplary and unusual aspect of the program, and the primary reason that we can talk about it today, is Mitchell's extensive and carefully detailed documentation of its fundamental procedures and processes.

FOLLOW THROUGH

Follow Through was a federally funded program of national scope. Initiated in 1966–1967, it followed on the success of Head Start. Although Head Start was and remains a most popular program, studies showed that the positive cognitive gains made by Head Start graduates washed

---

*Many of the curricular materials developed for the Workshop program can be found in the Lucy Sprague Mitchell Archives at Teachers College, Columbia University, New York.

out in subsequent years. This was attributed, at least partly, to the fact that the teaching in the elementary schools the children went to was counter to their more positive Head Start experience. The plan was to build upon Head Start by bringing comparable teaching techniques to the early elementary grades (kindergarten through third). From its inception Follow Through was a program of immense scope. As Zigler (1981) notes, it

> was planned to be both a large-scale ecological study of the effects of a variety of educational models for economically disadvantaged children and an attempt to extend the benefits of compensatory education for these children as they advanced through kindergarten and the primary grades. (p. xv)

In this review I draw on two sources, a presentation of the Bank Street Follow Through program in a volume describing the major program models (Gilkeson, Bowman, Smithberg, & Rhine, 1981) and a report of a study of the program based on interviews with staff and participants in many of the Bank Street Follow Through sites (Zimiles & Mayer, 1980).

Bank Street was one of the original sponsors/models of Follow Through and, under the direction of Elizabeth Gilkeson, worked in 13 sites of great ethnic, geographic, and ecological diversity, for instance, Brooklyn, N.Y.; Philadelphia, Pa.; Wilmington, Del.; Boulder, Colo.; Tuskegee, Ala.; Honolulu, Hawaii; and Fall River, Mass. In each site staff had to create relationships with school staff, both administrators and teachers, with parents, and with the community. In each site they had to find and develop working relationships with a local coordinator and a staff developer who would serve as liaison with the New York City based center. These staff were critical links to the local system. It is staggering to contemplate the hurdles of relating to the many personalities, styles, political contexts, cultures, and mores of the different communities, and finding ways of connecting to significant actors on the local scenes.

Richard Feldman (personal communication, April, 2000), who was associated with Follow Through from its planning stages, notes that a major strength of the program was that it represented "a way of looking at children and families in comprehensive terms, following the principles of the Head Start program." This broad-scope approach, taking account of child and family health and culture, and encouraging active participation in education, was new to most of the participating educators, as well as to some Bank Street staff.

From the beginning, Bank Street staff had a lot to learn. In the early months, the view was that "we had to educate them." This stance had to shift to an understanding that all had a lot to gain from each other. Many of the local principals and teachers were well educated and had had considerable experience in their jobs and high status in the community. Some had mixed feelings about being placed in a learner role. In the first years of the program, Bank Street staff was primarily White, whereas most of the target schools' population was not. This situation was counterproductive and had to change. A wide-ranging recruitment effort led to a staff of more varied backgrounds better suited to the diversity of the sites. The sheer size of the staff, their differing backgrounds, educational expertise, and styles of working required a lot of "working through" for all concerned. New staff had to develop commitments to what for some were new ideas, and in a parallel shift, old time Bank Streeters had to adapt and be willing to learn from those who were new to the enterprise but more knowledgeable about local mores and politics. To compound the issues further, Washington and the central Follow Through administration exerted considerable pressure on the sponsors to demonstrate "progress," to show that the program was succeeding in meeting its goals, and on the local sites to enact the model with fidelity.

These pressures may have led some staff to push teachers in the participant schools too hard. When asked about their experiences in Follow Through, some teachers expressed resentment at the Bank Street trainers, saying that they had been too arrogant, had "come on too strong." This response is paradoxical because the model emphasizes the importance of democratic process and nonauthoritarian personal interaction. In addition, tension may have resulted from the fact that the model requires extensive changes in attitudes as well as in practice. The absence of a recipe book puts additional stress on both trainer and trainee. A major attraction of explicit instructional methods is that they are easier to teach and easier to learn. The absence, in the Bank Street approach, of specific instructional materials or itemized lesson plans is both a fundamental strength and a serious weakness. The approach represents a way of thinking, a set of values, a disposition but not a prescription, not a list of dos and don'ts. Some people are attracted to guidelines that offer room for individual flexibility, but others find the lack of specific directives discomfiting, an issue that will continue to affect any new effort to change ways of working with children, teachers, administrators, and parents. It is perhaps partially the reason that teachers are more able to change how they arrange their rooms, the materials they provide, the mechanics of scheduling, and even the way they talk about the children than to make basic changes in their teaching. This phenomenon, observed in Follow Through, is echoed in reports from New Beginnings.

As time went on, sponsors and local sites came to share an understanding that they were part of a massive and federally funded social experiment. The Follow Through program was the subject of extensive evaluation. Each model/sponsor was funded to conduct research on its own program; some of the work of the Bank Street program is summarized in Gilkeson et al., 1981. Summative national evaluations were conducted by Stanford Research Institute, the Huron Institute, and Abt Associates. Apparently, few were pleased with the findings, and the publication of the evaluation results led to a small library of critiques and rebuttals. (For a comprehensive and incisive reprise of the issues, see House, Glass, McLean, & Walker, 1978.)

A point that surfaced repeatedly was the nature, adequacy, and appropriateness of the measures used to gauge program success. Although all participants may agree that they want students to "do well," to "succeed," definitions of what these terms mean vary widely. A program that includes a broad range of pedagogic approaches necessarily implies a range of desirable outcomes. Some are more difficult to assess than others. The easiest are those assessed by tests of achievement and factual knowledge. Models like Direct Instruction that focus on raising reading and math scores and the learning skills measured in standard achievement tests fared best in the evaluation. Those like Bank Street's that emphasize not only the importance of basic skills but also the centrality of developing long-term positive attitudes about learning and about schooling came out less well. There were no appropriate measures for these goals. In addition, the researchers paid little attention to how well the different sites implemented the different programs. Fidelity of implementation is of vital importance in assessing outcome, and little work had or has been devoted to this.

All of the problems associated with the Follow Through evaluation characterize evaluation efforts today as well as those of 20 years ago. Although people may be more aware of the issues and the technology has improved, the basic stumbling block has to do with values, that is, what is most important for children to learn and when should they have to know it. Further, discussion about teachers' preparation was minimum, and there was no analysis of what teachers need to know or want to accomplish in their work. Since there are fundamental disagreements among educators, politicians, and parents, we could echo the title of the report on the Follow Through evaluation by House et al. (1978): There is *no simple answer.*

THE LIMITS OF SCHOOL-BASED INTERVENTIONS

This brief recapitulation of two intervention programs carried out in earlier years by Bank Street staff has been offered in an effort to provide a historical perspective that can inform current and future work in the schools. In order to learn from experience, it is necessary to analyze past actions and reflect on their meaning.

Attempting to effect changes in school systems is hard work. But it is equally true that much satisfaction can be gained on all sides. No one can circumvent all of the problems. In many cases the mandate for change comes not from the grass roots but from high administration, although the grass-roots level is the focus of the change efforts. Similarly, there will always be some who relish and some who resent; there will always be some staff who can and some who cannot work with active or passive resistance.

The two programs described, the New York City Public School Workshop program and Bank Street sponsorship of the Follow Through program, were, as noted, very different in scope. Nevertheless, they share certain features; perhaps most important, they meet the criteria for program design and implementation put forth by Henrich et al. (1999). Each was firmly grounded in a theoretical base; each included multiple components and involved a wide range of relevant actors rather than a narrowly defined target population; and each spanned several years, enabling cumulative long-term effects as well as providing a chance for staff to learn on the job. As mentioned, the Workshop program was never formally evaluated. The national evaluation of Follow Through has been a subject of dispute as to the relevance of the evaluative measures for many of the sponsors. The program had a different impact on each site and teacher, probably not an unusual situation. And in each case the program's staying power—its life after the sponsors left—varied from site to site.

The institutionalization of a program, the ultimate goal of change efforts, is insufficiently addressed in the literature. These questions are poignantly raised, however, in an evaluation of Vision 21, a collaboration between Bank Street College and the Pittsburgh Public Schools to bring integrated social studies curriculum to six elementary schools. The 3-year evaluation focused on its positive impact on teachers, children, and the school administration, and notes that five of the six schools intended to continue the program after Bank Street's role was over. But a majority of teachers were concerned about funding, money for field trips and supplies, as well as about continued support from administrators and other teachers (Education Resources Group, 1996). In addition, time for teachers to meet together, and to plan, must be made part of the schedule. Although it is common knowledge that change is slow, labor intensive, and expensive, few are willing to underwrite the long-term costs necessary to sustain staff development initiatives.

In thinking about the power and the value of intervention efforts, especially those targeted to the schools, it is crucial to emphasize that most such efforts are usually directed to people who live in poverty, and poor families have many problems that the school cannot solve. Some of these can have direct impact on the program, such as significant mobility of poor families that leads to high turnover in the student population. In addition, some poor families welcome but others distrust the schools because they represent mainstream society. There is a paradox inherent in trying to bring sophisticated teaching to some schools housed in buildings that have broken windows, leaking ceilings, flaking paint, old-fashioned heating systems, no cooling systems, minimal libraries or none, and antiquated equipment. In short, much more extensive societal change has to take place before there can be true equity in education. That, however, does not preclude taking whatever action is feasible to make all schools safe, attractive, vital centers for learning and intellectual and personal growth.

Finally, we consistently advocate one's learning from experience but do not always practice our precept. Perhaps by documenting an important and extensive effort to affect educational practice, this book can serve the valuable purpose of helping others to minimize avoidable error and build on what we have learned from the past.

Acknowledgments. I want to thank Harriet K. Cuffaro, Richard Feldman, Nancy Nager, and Elaine Wickens for helpful comments on an earlier version of this chapter.

3

Interview with Catherine M. McFarland, Executive Officer, The Victoria Foundation

INTERVIEW BY CAROL LIPPMAN

Cathy McFarland is the executive officer of the Victoria Foundation, the largest and first funder of Project New Beginnings. This interview, conducted by Carol Lippman at the offices of the foundation, was designed to elicit Cathy's perspective on Newark and, in particular, the fortunes of public education in that city over the last four decades.

CAROL: I am curious, how did you first become interested in Newark?

CATHY: I grew up in the town of Bloomfield, which borders Newark. Newark was the destination of choice for shopping and services. Stores were plentiful, medical services were excellent, and the public library and museum were prized resources.

As an adult I became a member of the Episcopal Church in Bloomfield. In 1968, I joined our local minister in the Palm Sunday March sponsored by a group of Newark women who were members of the Queen of Angels Church there. They had formed an organization called Peace for Understanding. Father Linder, who was later to found the New Community Corporation, was a priest in that parish and, along with several other clergymen, gave support and encouragement to the organizers. People from Newark and the suburbs marched in the streets to show that there was broad solidarity for justice in the city.

That same year we also moved from Bloomfield to Montclair. As a young wife and mother, I became active in the Montclair Public Schools. The deep racial divisions that I saw there astonished me. Along with a number of other parents, I worked on integration issues in the Montclair community. Using magnet schools, Montclair ended up becoming a model district for school integration. In 1971, as a result of my involvement in the quest for racial equality in schools, the Victoria Foundation asked me to join its staff.

CAROL: Did both Blacks and Whites participate in the Palm Sunday March?

CATHY: Yes. It gave me a better understanding of what had happened in Newark during the summer riots of 1967. Then I was scared and didn't have enough personal contacts in the city to understand what was going on.

CAROL: What was the condition of the schools at the time of the riots?

CATHY: The schools were in terrible shape. I worked as a secretary for the New Jersey Education Association in 1962 during the struggle between the New Jersey Educational Association and the Newark Teacher's Union to represent the teachers. The NJEA was documenting the condition of the schools for some time, and I learned then how bad things were. In fact, in 1963 NJEA asked the governor to take over the schools. There was great animosity between the NJEA and the NTU. At that time, NJEA wouldn't use the word *union*—they were a "professional organization." NJEA lost the election and that ended their involvement in Newark. The worsening conditions in the schools and the lack of respect for parents became another ember that ultimately fueled the riots.

Victoria Foundation's involvement with Newark schools began in 1963–1964. The trustees were exploring potential areas of foundation support. Bob Lilly, who at that time was president of New Jersey Bell and a trustee of the Victoria Foundation, suggested that the lack of access to quality education and job opportunity within the city was a critical problem. It was then that the trustees turned their attention to education with the formation of the Cleveland Victoria Project at Cleveland School.

CAROL: Did you work with only one school?

CATHY: We were discouraged, actually threatened, from expanding to a second school by the teacher's union. Ultimately, however, it was the politics within the Newark Board of Education that caused the foundation to terminate the program. There was no accountability.

CAROL: What was Victoria's ongoing funding position?

CATHY: The foundation stopped funding the Newark Public Schools in 1983. We directed grants to independent schools, parochial schools, and enrichment programs that worked within the public schools, but the funding did not go directly to the board. There was one exception, the Harriet Tubman School. It was a true community school and the foundation supported their efforts for a number of years.

We began funding again after the state takeover. There was no question in our minds that the quality of Newark's public education and the revitalization of the city were intertwined.

CAROL: Living conditions in Newark had deteriorated pretty badly by that time as well.

CATHY: The city went through various waves of arson, including arson for profit as well as for neglect. One could follow the arson for profit because a house would turn over at an increased price two or three times, then all of a sudden there would be a fire. This happened in the neighborhoods throughout the city as well as the neighborhood surrounding the Cleveland School. It is really wonderful to see the Cleveland neighborhood today. The squalid conditions of high-rise public housing complexes have been replaced by new low-rise developments.

The arson of the 1970s was devastating. However, the continued neglect of public housing had caused intolerable conditions. Elevators within the buildings never worked and more than 1,500 children lived in the small area where the housing stood.

Community groups were unsuccessful in getting the housing authority to address these conditions. Eventually, in the 1980s, the housing authority began to vacate units and eventually imploded many of the projects. Victoria supported the New Jersey Legal Services in their efforts to require the city to replace the housing. A landmark decision was rendered that required the housing authority to replace, one-for-one, the destroyed units. Many units have been replaced, but there are still many to go. The court left it open for the Coalition for Affordable Housing to return if the city did not live up to the mandate of the decision.

CAROL: I wonder if the biggest effect of that decision to implode the public housing was simply to move the lowest socioeconomic group out of the city?

CATHY: The movement out of the city began much earlier. When the Columbus Homes were closed, many families moved in with relatives or moved into structures that were not legal multifamily residences. Others left for the Oranges and Irvington. I think the movement out of the city was not due to the destruction of the projects but was rather the result of the economic decline begun in the 1950s and the earlier deterioration of neighborhoods.

CAROL: In 1995, when I took my first trip into Newark by car, it was a burned-out city full of rubble. I thought, "My God, this looks like pictures of London after the war."

CATHY: You are right. Little had been done by 1995, a few pockets of new housing and the beginnings of the New Jersey Performing Arts Center. Along with the museums and the universities, it was NJPAC that gave impetus to the downtown transformation.

In 1985, the Prudential Insurance Company first took the leadership and formed the Newark Collaboration Group, made up of business leaders, foundations, and community organizations. It eventually spun off the Newark Education Council.

Most important, we worked behind the scenes to get the city to give a parcel of land to a group called Vogue Housing. They built the first new housing units: University Heights in the Central Ward. That attracted for-profit developers who began to invest in the city for the first time. Before that, the only new housing was built by nonprofits, usually after a fight with the city to get land. The mayor said outright that he didn't want any more poor people in the city, so why build more housing for them? The Newark Economic Development Corporation hoarded large blocks of land and wouldn't let go of them. Now, that land is being developed with private housing. In addition, Route 78, anticipated for a number of years in the South Ward, had a negative impact on the surrounding neighborhood.

CAROL: So they all sold?

CATHY: The middle class didn't invest in their houses. Then by the time the state announced the actual location of the highway and bought out all the houses along the path, the neighborhood had deteriorated. The highway divided the Weequahic section from the rest of the South Ward.

CAROL: Were people in that neighborhood sending their children to public schools?

CATHY: Yes, they were. The Weequahic section was a Jewish neighborhood that had some of the finest schools in America.

CAROL: I just finished reading Philip Roth's *Patrimony*. He talks about going to 13th Avenue School.

CATHY: Right. Maple Avenue School, 13th Avenue School, and Weequahic High School all boast well-known graduates. Barringer High School was very well regarded. It really is hard to see how things have changed. However, if you study the city, the decline didn't really start with the '67 riots. It was a combination of factors over the years.

CATHY: When Jim Florio was in his last year as governor, Mary Lee Fitzgerald, the state commissioner of education, and a squad of New Jersey Department of Education people descended upon the Newark Public Schools and the Board of Education offices. They just seized all the files. I have been told that there was information in those files that might have convicted everyone from the superintendent to members of the board of education. That information has never surfaced and, to my knowledge, no one has ever been arrested or charged on the basis of evidence in those files. When Whitman became governor, the new commissioner of education instituted the takeover of the schools.

This was really heartening to those of us who had watched as the children of Newark were cheated out of a quality education. But the law required only that the board of education and top administrators be removed. It didn't go far enough. The legislation should have had a lot more power, for example, to enable the state-appointed superintendent to throw out all the contracts that the board had made with the union. But it didn't. When Beverly Hall [the first state-appointed superintendent] came in, she had her work cut out for her. I think she did an incredible job within her short tenure.

CAROL: How did Victoria get involved with Dr. Hall?

CATHY: The Foundation asked her about her first priorities. She outlined specific areas in which she needed support: restructuring school/corporate management, school/community partnership, and parent leadership performance. We pledged $1 million for 5 years. Dr. Hall wanted to have New Beginnings in every single K–3 classroom in the district. We also funded CTAC [Community Training and Assistance Center] to help the superintendent develop school-based management.

Remember, before Dr. Hall got here, Newark's schools and its public works system were employment systems rather than education and government systems. Why did that happen? It happened because of racism. There were no employment opportunities in Newark in the banks or any major corporations. The only place one could get a job, if you were Black and poor, was within the public schools or within the city government. It was very much about patronage. It didn't just start with Mayor Gibson. That was just the way city politics worked.

CAROL: Now I understand why the community was up in arms when Beverly Hall came in as State district superintendent of schools and started cleaning house.

CATHY: Beverly began by laying off cafeteria workers who had been employed by the district for years, some of whom were "no shows."

There was an article in the *New Jersey Reporter* about 12 years ago, maybe a little bit longer, about the Newark Public Schools, the board of education, and the money that was being spent just on cars and on fancy accessories. Nobody stood up and protested. Too many people were afraid of losing their jobs.

CAROL: The city has a history of corruption, from what you're saying, that goes back way before the riots. Were the riots merely symptomatic of an oppressive situation?

CATHY: More than the riots, I think the strike by teachers a few years earlier had the most critical implications for education. The teachers were out a very long time.

CAROL: What happened to the children?

CATHY: Well, they didn't go to school. There were some temporary classrooms set up in churches. Many good teachers were lost to the system and people moved away from the city. The riots were only the ultimate explosion of long-simmering frustration.

CAROL: We're talking about a history of over 30 years of educational neglect. And it's only been 5 since the state takeover.

CATHY: That does not mean that there weren't committed teachers and principals in Newark—there were. There also were some schools where you knew quality education was occurring, such as the Harriet Tubman School, but they were few and far between. There was no administrative support for educational excellence.

Beverly Hall was the first person I heard speak about putting children first. Children just never got mentioned before she came. She also encouraged parents to get involved again. That hadn't happened for many, many years. In the 1970s, I remember meeting with the organizers of a successful rent strike at the Stella Wright Public Housing. I asked one of the women, "Where are your sending schools [schools that send children to the high schools]?" She replied, "Oh, we have five different sending schools." I asked her if she was involved with these schools. She looked at me as if I was out of my mind and said, "What do you mean?" I said, "Well, you've been so effective in getting things changed in public housing, winning a judgment against the housing authority and the city, which I think is far more difficult than talking to a principal." Then she declared simply enough, "We can't go to the schools." I asked her why, and she said they would not listen. So, the history of the schools is one in which the parents were not welcome, whether it was said out loud or through a locked door.

CAROL: Were these parents who had gone through the Newark Public Schools themselves?

CATHY: Yes! Some of them were in fact knowledgeable and could have changed things around.

CAROL: Given this history, it was a courageous move on Beverly's part to set up Parents Academies in every school to bring parents in.

CATHY: Telling the principals that they were going to be judged on how they related to the community took nerve. No one had ever said that before in Newark, at least in the last 30 years.

CAROL: Clearly with small children, we know that you can't ignore the parents without a terrible cost.

CATHY: Then too the advent of crack cocaine in the 1980s took a terrible toll on the city. Poor families that had previously been able to stay together, often with the help of grandparents, could no longer do so. The sense of despair became overwhelming, and more and more children seemed to be raising themselves. They came into the schools with so much going on in their lives. I don't know that anybody could do anything to change things for them other than keep them there overnight.

CAROL: On top of crack cocaine came the AIDS epidemic. An entire generation of parents was lost, and the children were left with grandparents and even great grandparents to raise them.

CATHY: Mary Bennett, who was principal at Shebazz High School, told me that one year she lost 18 mothers between September and December alone.

CAROL: To AIDS?

CATHY: That's what I thought, but she said that it was not completely due to the epidemic. Some of it was hypertension, lack of medical attention, and depression. Mary Bennett was concerned with how to help children cope with grief.

CAROL: The problems of the educational system are the problems of a city in decline.

CATHY: As much as Victoria was doing in the independent, parochial, and alternative schools, we could potentially reach only 4,000 children. There were 43,000 children in public schools. If we were going to significantly change lives, we had to be in the public schools. Yet we knew it was to no avail during the previous administrations because the resources didn't get used in appropriate ways. When the state took over the schools, the foundation board of trustees and the education committee felt that there was a window of opportunity to really make things better for all Newark's children. We knew that Dr. Hall faced strong opposition. If we didn't take a risk, the chance to make improvements would be lost.

Prudential got involved at about the same time. The Advocates, a group of civic leaders determined to put children first, was also formed. The Advocates are not just about supporting the public schools but about what is good for children.

CAROL: Do you think that all of this has made a difference?

CATHY: Yes. There is a new professionalism in the schools. There is accountability. I have been very pleased with the Bank Street results. I also feel good about what the Victoria Foundation has done since the takeover to improve the capacity of teachers, principals, and administrators. I think that regardless of the future leadership, our accomplishments won't have been for naught.

CAROL: As you are talking, I am thinking about some of our original 16 teachers who have left the classroom to work in the Office of Early Childhood and with the Office of Literacy. They are not just affecting 27 children but an entire district. That is how you hope to make lasting change.

CATHY: At Montclair State College, we funded Project Thistle to support graduate education students. And that's how Marion Bolden got her advanced degree. Now she is superintendent of schools. I am confident that over the years we have had a big impact on the Newark schools and Bank Street has been one of the many important players in our efforts. We could not have done it alone. I think the future is looking good for the children of Newark for the first time in many, many years.

4

Newark in Context

JONATHAN G. SILIN AND CAROL LIPPMAN

In this chapter the editors place the Newark–Bank Street collabora-
tion in context, beginning with a brief overview of the history of
Newark and public education in that city. They also locate Project
New Beginnings within the major streams of school-reform research
and practice. New Jersey was the first state to mandate widespread
adoption of Comprehensive School Reform for all of its 30 resource-
poor and low-achieving districts. Silin and Lippman discuss the
challenges such a requirement poses for those already working on
the front lines of school reform.

S CHOOLS ARE ONE OF THE MOST CONTENTIOUS SCREENS
upon which Americans project their hopes and anxieties, their
dreams and discontents. Schools are approached as panaceas and
function as the scapegoats for an impossibly broad range of social problems from poverty and unemployment to teen pregnancy and HIV/AIDS.
They are sites of contradiction, which are imbued with powers to preserve the best of the past and prepare students for an unknown future. It
is little wonder that educators are often torn in too many directions,
their work fragmented by divergent demands. It's little wonder too that
someone or some group is always attempting to reform the schools,
promising to make them more efficient or more student-centered, more
rational or more responsive to contemporary social conditions.

When the courts intervene and require state supervision of local
schools, as they did in 1995 in Newark, arguing that the district was
failing to provide a "thorough and efficient" education as mandated by

the New Jersey constitution, then everyone must take note. Even those who oppose such a radical step with its imposition of centralized control and indictment of local governance will acknowledge that something is terribly wrong and that extraordinary remedies are needed. But what exactly went wrong in Newark and, given the complexity of schools in the postmodern world, what kinds of remedies will prove most effective?

Although the extensive reports of the New Jersey Department of Education written in the decade prior to the takeover detail extensive corruption, administrative inefficiency, and poor student performance, we were not ourselves present in the district at that time. Nor is it easy to identify simple cause-and-effect patterns in large systems, especially when they are buffeted by the winds of economic decline and dramatic population shifts. We can write more confidently, however, about the remedy New Beginnings hoped to provide by referring to the overriding sense of moral purpose that fueled the project's work (Fullan, 1999). In the simplest terms, our goal was to help the schools make a difference in the life chances of individual students. From a societal perspective, we wanted to nurture the social capital—commitment, practices, and habits of mind that are needed to make democracy function in an ever more ethnically and racially diverse country—and to develop the intellectual capital required in a world where globalization and rapidly changing technological environments have become the norm.

Schools are inevitably embedded in a series of overlapping contexts. The unique story of Newark tells of the socioeconomic forces that have shaped education in that city. The broader history of education speaks to the many myths—merit, efficiency, progress, and the value of market economies in education—that have buoyed the American faith in schools and masked harsher realities of privilege, racial injustice, and fragmentation of communities (Oakes & Lipton, 1999). The current political moment—with its emphasis on standards, high-stakes testing, and accountability—tells of the increasing public demands under which contemporary school people try to effect change.

In this chapter we briefly explore these contextual variables and locate New Beginnings in the landscape of school reform. When reviewing the final drafts of the essays composing this volume, we were struck by the way that each of the authors sang a different song and yet shared a common melody, a melody that is the city of Newark itself—a once prosperous industrial hub of the 19th century seeking to make a comeback as a center of business and commerce in the 21st century.

CITY OF IMMIGRANTS, INDUSTRY, AND INFAMY

Newark is a city made both famous and infamous during the summer of 1967 when the governor of New Jersey called upon the National Guard to quell the riots that broke out after decades of economic downturn and dramatic demographic shifts. The "weekend warriors," however, did more than clear the streets of angry looters and close the city off to incoming food and supplies. Buried amongst photographs of armed troops patrolling the streets, smashed storefronts, and angry Black militants demanding more jobs and better housing are images of another Newark. This is the city that was a thriving seat of business and industry, providing a fifth of all jobs and paying one quarter of all industrial wages in New Jersey, during the late 19th and early 20th centuries (Anyon, 1997). In 1967 New Jersey's largest city, a 19th-century haven for European immigrants, first Irish and German, later Italians and Russian Jews, became an emblem for the pent-up discontent of America's urban poor, for the deep veins of racial injustice that run just below the surface of daily life.

Four decades after the riots, Newark has become a city of prodigious redevelopment. From the stunning New Jersey Performing Arts Center to the Market Street office buildings with their high ceilings and elaborate stonework exteriors refitted for technology-intensive businesses, the city is finally experiencing its long-awaited revival. The streets of the Ironbound, once primarily a Portuguese community, lined with small bakeries, restaurants, and clothing shops, are increasingly filled with young artists and entrepreneurs drawn from New York City by lower rents and a more reasonable way of life. In neighborhoods of the Central Ward, brick and white clapboard one- and two-family homes are slowly replacing the anonymous, high-rise projects that urban planners cite as a cause of antisocial behavior in the urban ghetto. There is a vitality and optimism in the new Newark that reflects years of planning by civic and business leaders, religious organizations, and private philanthropies.

To be sure, the landscape of Newark still bears the visible scars of the 1967 riots and their aftermath—square-block rubble-strewn lots that once contained crime-ridden housing projects, boarded-up apartment buildings that await renovations along major thoroughfares such as Clinton Avenue, and superhighways that now crisscross the city, destroying once prosperous and coherent neighborhoods of the South Ward. Less visible but all the more troubling are the statistics on the financial and physical health of Newark's families. These suggest that the root causes of the riots—racism, unemployment, substance abuse, inadequate education, and social services—have hardly been eliminated. A third of the city residents still live in poverty, the 9.2% rate of unemployment is double the state average, and, despite a gain in total housing units between 1992 and 2000, the rate of home ownership fell by 3% (Jacobs, 2002). Newark also ranks among the worst U.S. cities in terms of AIDS, lead paint poisoning, and tuberculosis. With respect to children, 82% receive free or reduced lunches and the city, with 3% of New Jersey's population, contains slightly more than 20% of all children who live in families receiving Aid to Families With Dependent Children (AFDC)/Temporary Assistance to Needy Families (TANF) and not quite 20% of children receiving food stamps (Association for Children of New Jersey, 2000). In terms of health care, Newark children fare little better—13.2% of children are born with low birth weight versus 7.7% statewide, 8.1% of births occur without any prenatal care versus 1.2% statewide; and there is a 13.3% infant mortality per 1,000 births versus 6.3% statewide.

During much of the 19th and early 20th centuries, Newark's school system grew rapidly to meet the needs of the immigrants who filled the working-class neighborhoods of the Central Ward. In the forefront of public education, the city's innovative programs included extensive kindergartens, the Gary plan for extended days, all-year schools, summer schools, and vocational/trade education. The district was one of the first in the country to establish a bureau of child guidance and a reference and research unit. Anyon (1997) argues that the decline of the Newark Public Schools began only in the late 1920s when the city started to lose industrial jobs as well as middle- and upper-class elites to the surrounding suburbs. In succeeding decades the long-term impact of the Great Depression, the reliance on property taxes to finance public education throughout the state, and economic decline continued to negatively affect the district's physical plants and programs. Despite the federal policy that supported suburbanization rather than investment in cities, large-scale local patronage and corruption, and declining teacher standards (1 out of 3 teachers were long-term substitutes), the schools of the 1950s are still remembered by some as places that offered a ladder out of poverty for the poorest families and a way to enter the middle class for those who came from the working classes (see chaps. 1 and 6).

Although Newark experienced large-scale emigration just before World War I, the most dramatic demographic changes occurred immediately after World War II as African Americans left the South to escape poverty, segregation, and inadequate education. In 1961, over a third of Newark's population was African-American, up from 10.7% in 1940.

By 1998, the school population was 65% African-American, 25% Hispanic, and 10% White (Community Training and Assistance Center, 2000). The continuing loss of entry-level industrial jobs to surrounding suburban communities, patterns of employment discrimination, and restrictive educational requirements made it difficult for many of the most recently arrived to find work.

During the 1960s, Newark was not the only New Jersey school district lacking the resources to face growing social problems, declining student achievement, and mounting public criticism. Beginning in 1973, a long series of court cases challenged the funding of public education across the state. In that year, the courts (*Robinson v. Cahill*) upheld the argument that a primary reliance on local property taxes for school financing led to unequal educational opportunities for children in property-poor districts and was thus a violation of the state's constitution. Although challenges to property tax financing were raised in 42 states between 1970 and 1995, in 1990 (*Abbott v. Burke*) New Jersey became the first to go so far as to rule that poorer urban students were entitled to *more* school aid than were other students. In response to a stream of litigation, the New Jersey State Legislature passed the Public School Education Act of 1975 that set up procedures to assure that local districts were in compliance with the court rulings. During the 1980s, state monitoring was continuously tightened, and in 1988 the legislature passed the State Operation of a School/District Act enabling the takeover of districts that were "unwilling or unable" to comply with state certification requirements.

The State Takeover

Beginning in 1984 and continuing until the takeover 11 years later, the Newark Public Schools consistently failed to meet state monitoring standards. In 1993, a state report concluded that "the Newark School District has been at best flagrantly delinquent and at worst deceptive in discharging its obligations to the children enrolled" (Community Training and Assistance Center, 2000). The state takeover of the district officially began in 1995 with the appointment by the state commissioner of education of a new school superintendent, Beverly Hall, and a new board of advisors (13 appointed by the commissioner and 2 by the City of Newark) to replace the old board of education. The new superintendent was, among other things, required to evaluate all central office administrators, reorganize the central administration, report regularly to the New Jersey Board of Education and the new board of advisors, conduct on-site evaluations of all principals and vice-principals, and increase parent, teacher, and community involvement. When approached by the Victoria Foundation about how it might support her efforts, Hall, who had most recently been deputy chancellor of the New York City Public Schools, responded that among her top priorities was bringing Bank Street into the schools to restructure early childhood education (see chaps. 3 and 5). Thus began the conversations out of which Project New Beginnings was born and became a key component of Hall's 5-year plan for improving education in Newark.

During the 1990s, state takeovers became an increasingly popular, if extreme, vehicle for prompting school reform. By the end of the decade, 24 states had passed legislation enabling takeovers. In 1989, Jersey City was the first state takeover, and 10 years later Newark was one of 19 districts encompassing 1 million students and 1,500 schools under state control across the country.

Whereas the New Jersey legislation calls for the replacement of top administrators, other states allow administrators to remain in office or place the district directly under the mayor's control. No matter what the specific process, the outcomes in most districts have been far from encouraging for the takeover strategy (School Reform News, 1999; Ziebarth, 2001). Overall, there have been more successes in addressing dysfunctions in administrative and budgetary management than in addressing student achievement. Nonetheless, in 1999, 4 years into the state takeover, Newark itself experienced a $73 million funding gap that precipitated a serious fiscal crisis and a round of finger-pointing and lawsuits between the city and state (Reid, 2001).

A comprehensive report on the impact of the state takeover suggests that the majority of stakeholders—teachers, students, parents, and local administrators—believe that there has been an overall improvement in the elementary and middle schools (Community Assistance and Training Center, 2000). This improvement includes better school climate and conditions for learning, increased parent and community involvement, and refashioned planning processes. Although the renewed focus on student achievement has led to uneven results on standardized tests, attendance has risen across the district (Johnston, 2000). The report, however, faults the district for failing to define its priorities and exercise effective leadership, lacking an adequate data management system that would allow for effective accountability, demonstrating continued operational problems, and failing to make sufficient progress in improving the high schools. Troubling too are the lack of benchmarks that determine when student achievement and administrative restructuring have proceeded far enough to permit a return to local control (see chap. 5). Courts are hard pressed to identify what remedies are required if a district under state control is unable to improve student performance and what measures must be taken by the district to prevent backsliding once progress has been made.

Progressive Education as School Reform

Tyack and Cuban (1995) suggest that the history of American education is best written as the story of continuing efforts to reform a system that could never live up to the hopes with which it was endowed by parents and the practical, although often contradictory, demands it was asked to meet by politicians and policymakers. The first advocates of free, universal, and compulsory education, like Horace Mann and Henry Barnard, were in a sense only reformers, who wanted to create a coherent system out of the existing network of local schools. Their goals were clear: to preserve the "common" culture and to assure economic and social stability through education that makes everyone a stakeholder in the status quo. At the end of the 19th century, a second group of reformers, the administrative progressives, sought to further rationalize a system overburdened with successive waves of immigrant groups that threatened "the American" way of life. The schools were to run like efficient factories with all children receiving an education commensurate with their abilities and potential employment.

During the first part of the 20th century, the pedagogical progressives initiated an additional set of curricular reforms geared to produce adults who understood and would therefore participate in the democratic process. Informal, active classrooms, saturated with socially relevant curriculum and led by teachers responsive to the social, emotional, and cognitive needs of their students, were the hallmark of the small, private schools that were the vanguard of the progressive movement. Although the ultimate influence of the pedagogical progressives on mainstream institutions is still debated by educational historians (Cremin, 1961; Ravitch, 2000), it was only the cold war that revived public interest in how teaching and learning actually proceeds in classrooms. Then a heightened concern about national security, symbolically triggered by the 1957 launching of Sputnik, brought a round of curricular reforms to increase our scientific and economic competitiveness in the new world order. At the same time, the 1960s civil rights movement brought a renewed focus on the inequities of a school system that functioned to reinforce the status quo and failed to right social injustice by fostering real social mobility.

Since the 1960s, the pace of reform, if not tangible achievements, has quickened. Beyond the ad hoc assimilation of new curriculum materials, program initiatives, and organizational modifications, Fink and Stoll (1998) suggest four major streams of research-based approaches to school reform. Each of the successive approaches—effective schools, school improvement, restructuring, and reculturing schools—has added to our fund of knowledge about how school change occurs. Each too has its dedicated proponents. However, it is hard to find sustained evidence that any one stream of research/practice has dramatically changed the everyday "grammar of schooling" or that sufficient attention has been given to questions of power and equity in the reform process (Elmore, 1995; Slee, Weiner, & Tomlinson, 1998).

PROJECT NEW BEGINNINGS

Although Project New Beginnings does not fit easily within the Fink and Stoll typology, the geography they chart helps to illuminate the strengths and weaknesses with which it entered the field of school reform. Based on the developmental-interaction approach (Nager & Shapiro, 2000; Shapiro & Biber, 1972), the project has its roots in the experimental progressive tradition of the early 20th century. Here the soil is fortified by the writings of social philosophers such as John Dewey and George Counts, educators like Lucy Sprague Mitchell and Charlotte Windsor, and a raft of child development specialists who help teachers keep track of how children can learn in age-appropriate ways. With the commitment to the amelioration of social ills through the application of scientific principles, this is a thoroughly modernist philosophy with no room for the fragmentation, uncertainty, and multiple narratives that permeate postmodern thought. Rather than relying on a wide purview of how systems and cultures change, previous Bank Street interventions have drawn on an older, more tightly focused vision of staff development that seeks to shift the ways that teachers organize their classrooms, interact with children, and structure learning experiences (see chap. 2). The strength of such an approach is its attention to the individual needs, interests, and learning styles of adults and children. As a Newark teacher reviewed her first year in the project, she summarized the approach this way:

> I guess it was like teaching the whole child. They were teaching all of us. They weren't just teaching our head and our ideas. They were teaching our hearts. . . . I can't separate them.

Change occurs through the all too human process of building trusting relationships one encounter at a time. In Newark, for example, the core of the program during the first 4 years was the labor-intensive pairing of teachers with staff developers who visited classrooms several times each month to observe, work with individuals and groups of children, and introduce new materials and teaching strategies. Without a predetermined template marking stages of change or a fixed curriculum toward which to aspire, the developmental-interaction approach leaves ample latitude for individual teacher initiative. This problem-solving, inquiry-based paradigm requires teachers to translate broad principles into their local practices. It is the very opposite of the "training" or knowledge consumption model that often takes shape through a set of discrete workshops focusing on building a repertoire of specific teaching behaviors (Little, 1993).

While the developmental-interaction model respects the subtleties and uncertainties of classroom life, as well as the unique histories and circumstances of teachers, the project's experience confirms that it can leave some teachers without a clear sense of achievable goals (Schwartz & Silin, 1998). Teachers wanting more explicit guidance because of either their cultural histories and/or individual learning styles may be frustrated by the lack of specificity (see chap. 14). During an early project meeting, a staff developer encapsulates this perspective and her frustration, noting, "When a teacher says, 'Am I doing it wrong?' I want to say we are not talking about right or wrong. It's how you look at kids." This deceptively simple complaint masks the complexity of the discourse in which looking at kids is embedded. Along with the language of developmentally appropriate curriculum are all of the practices, emotions, and the culturally specific categories that give meaning to the work of progressive educators (McNaughton, 2000). After 3 years in the project, a committed New Beginnings teacher articulates her understanding of the discourse this way:

> Bank Street has opened my eyes to exactly the way children learn and think. . . . I listen to children now. I have a different ear. I am not interested in the right answer. I am interested in how did you get there, your thinking. I am constantly watching, trying to figure out what's going on inside that little head. . . . I want to know what's driving you, what's making you go.

Over time the New Beginnings staff development model was modified to include courses, workshops, and study groups geared to building instructional skills as well as to exploring the foundational ideas of progressive pedagogy. These structural changes reflected the growth of the project, its commitment to building capacity in the district and to providing more opportunities for teachers who learn most effectively away from their own classrooms (Putnam & Borko, 2000). At the same time, project staff became more precise in defining goals and objectives with teachers and project leadership increasingly directed its attention to working with the district administration to assure an overall environment that supported inquiry-based pedagogy.

Although many of the newer approaches to school reform emphasize either the politics/structural impediments to system change or the culture of the individual school and district, New Beginnings emphasized the central role of the teacher in achieving changes that affect student outcomes (Datnow & Costellano, 2000). Fullan (1991) puts it most succinctly: "Change in education depends upon what teachers do and think—it's as simple and complex as that" (p. 117).

Unfortunately, the realities of daily life often undercut this "simple and complex" dictum of effective practice. In Newark teachers must be familiar with the New Jersey Core Curriculum Content Standards, the curriculum guides published by the district itself, and the demands of the Comprehensive School Reform initiative adopted by the school. The goals, objectives, and activities of all curriculum planning must be rationalized within these frameworks. In addition, within any given year teachers must respond to a plethora of new programs, some such as New Beginnings and the Children's Literacy Initiative built into the district's 5-year plan and others emanating from the central Office of Teaching and Learning, which has separate directors for each of the major curriculum areas, including early childhood. This is not to find fault with a particular program but to draw attention to the cumulative impact on teachers and children of many uncoordinated curricular initiatives (Hargreaves, 1998).

New Beginnings has survived the frequent importation of new programs into its classrooms because the project has remained flexible and adaptable (Silin & Schwartz, 2000). This permeability, however, has not been without a cost. During the third year of the project, for example, New Beginnings staff developers worked alongside teachers to learn about the new district-mandated literacy assessments, assisted in their implementation, and, when necessary, advocated with principals and central office personnel for teachers swamped with demands. Research suggests that it was the structural changes already in place—the extensive use of learning centers, the dramatically increased use of individual and small-group as opposed to whole-group instruction, the more fluid, less fragmented use of time—that allowed teachers to administer the assessments. At the same time, with the intensive literacy focus, there was little time left for social studies, classroom discussions growing out of children's lives, and curriculum built on their immediate questions and concerns.

THE PROMISE OF COMPREHENSIVE SCHOOL REFORM

Given the already complex terrain of school reform in Newark—state standards, district curricula, outside program initiatives, and our own presence—New Beginnings staff were unsettled to learn that in the fall of 1998 the New Jersey Supreme Court required that every school in each of the 30 tax-poor Abbot districts, encompassing 450 schools, adopt a Comprehensive School Reform (CSR) model within 3 years. Just 3 years into its own efforts to bring major change to Newark's early childhood classrooms, the project was having its first measurable successes (Kopacsi & Hochwald, 1997; Kopacsi & Onsongo, 1999) and had begun to establish strong connections with the district's decision makers. The confusion that New Beginnings staff, teachers, and administrators experienced about why and how this new state mandate was to be carried out mirrored concerns throughout New Jersey's Abbot districts (Erlichson, Goertz, & Turnbull, 1999).

New Jersey was the first state to mandate comprehensive school reform on such a large scale. The ruling came as part of the fifth decision in the long-standing *Abbott v. Burke* school financing case. If schools did not choose among one of five specified models, then they were assigned to Success for All/Roots and Wings (SFA), a highly prescriptive, skills-based program developed by Robert Slavin and Nancy Madden. In short, SFA became the court-designated "presumptive" model for the state. In addition, schools were required to adopt a zero-based budget drawing on local, state, and federal revenues. For the first time, individual school budgets were to be submitted to the New Jersey Department of Education via the local district for approval.

Reform by fiat goes counter to the literature on CSR indicating that successful implementation occurs only if there is voluntary and widespread teacher buy-in. The court-ordered reform, currently being fought by the New Jersey Education and Law Center, reflects the national popularity of this latest educational panacea as well as the continuing deterioration in New Jersey's poorest districts. Developed during the 1990s, CSR models were created in response to the failure of piecemeal reforms in the 1980s when *A Nation at Risk* had warned that American schools were not producing a sufficiently skilled work force to compete in the world marketplace. By the mid-1990s, impatient to see results, judges and legislators found it hard to resist the sweeping promises of

CSR advocates. Here is what the Education Commission of the States (1999) says:

> Comprehensive school reform is not just another school improvement strategy—it is a significant leap forward in reforming today's public schools. Comprehensive school reform addresses all students, all academic subjects and all teachers. When done well, a school is overhauled from top to bottom. Adding one program on top of another is thrown out in favor of the much more difficult work of reorganizing schools, targeting professional development for teachers and principals, changing curriculum and making tough budget decisions. (p. 4)

Beyond the rhetoric and expansive claims, CSR was backed by federal legislation. In 1988 and 1994, Title I was broadened to support school-wide change projects, and in 1996–1997, funding eligibility for schools was lowered from 75% of children living in poverty to 50% making it easier for poor schools to adopt such projects. Then, in 1997, Congress created the Comprehensive School Reform Demonstration program, which enabled schools to apply for $50,000 grants for up to 3 years to assist in implementing CSR. The legislation came equipped with a list of 17 approved models, although it also left room for schools to develop their own.

In retrospect, one of the most striking aspects of the CSR phenomenon was the absence of rigorous evaluations indicating its positive impact on student learning (Desimore, 2000). Although some models had been evaluated by their own design teams, there was insufficient evidence to determine their effectiveness, let alone comparative data among the models. Following on lessons learned from earlier federal programs that showed critical differences in implementation within sites and among sites, initial studies focused on the extent of implementation as the necessary prerequisite to looking at ultimate questions of effectiveness.

In New Jersey, implementation of CSR has been rife with problems stemming from the extremely short time frame for compliance, lack of capacity, and unclear roles and responsibilities among all the components—schools, local districts, and the department of education (Erlichson & Goertz, 2001). Even CSR advocates note that some low-performing schools may lack the leadership, internal structures, and supportive culture necessary to make this kind of reform work (Education Commission of the States, 1999). Then both the State Department of Education and the models fell short of providing the assistance schools required for implementation. Finally, CSR involved a basic change in governance. Although the new zero-based budgets are to be constructed in the school and sent to the district office, the department of education ultimately approves them. The traditional linear hierarchy—school, district, department of education—is transformed into an arrangement that places the school in the middle and the principal juggling sometimes contradictory demands of the district and state.

Despite the claims of CSR proponents that these models would rationalize the school reform process by replacing the crazy quilt of programs that exist in many urban schools, such has not proven to be the case in many Newark schools. New Beginnings has made a concerted effort to collaborate with the models adopted by each of the schools with which it is working. In part, these collaborations have been successful because a majority of the CSR models place greater emphasis on matters of school governance than on the day-to-day realities of curriculum development. Ironically, the developmental-interaction approach did not warrant designation in the 1997 Comprehensive School Reform Development program (CSRD) legislation as a comprehensive school reform model nor does it have neatly packaged program components that make it easily replicable. Yet at its core is essential knowledge about how children and adults learn and the experience of developing relevant and mindful curriculum that can lead to permanent changes in how teachers teach and what their students learn.

State takeovers, court-mandated CSR, and the intricacies of school budgeting are not the subject matter of this volume. They do provide important knowledge about the context in which the Newark–Bank Street collaboration flourished. More fundamentally, they attest to the failure of American schools to treat all their students fairly and equally. Schools do not and cannot correct the painful disparities in resource distribution that plague our country. However, not to strive to make every classroom a more just community, one in which adults and children treat each other with respect and in which everyone is encouraged to reach his or her highest potential, is to deny our core responsibilities as educators. At the same time, we recognize that there are many institutions in a child's life that educate—family, religion, community, and the media. Acknowledging these realities, we hold schools accountable as a critical site where children can learn to make sense of their experience and where they can equip themselves with the skills, ideas, and vision necessary to bring about a better future.

5

The Challenges of School Reform

Beverly L. Hall

Beverly Hall, the first court-appointed state district superintendent of Newark, provides a firsthand account of the difficulties she faced fulfilling the state mandates for reform. She is critical of the state takeover legislation, the city unions, and the entrenched bureaucracy she found in the central office. Although Hall herself is a staunch supporter of progressive education, she encountered strong resistance from others. This essay offers an important lesson about the ways that reform can be challenged from within the system despite leadership at the very top. Hall is currently the head of the Atlanta school system.

LOW STUDENT PERFORMANCE and low academic standards were among the gravest deficiencies leading to the State of New Jersey's take over of the Newark Public Schools. Many years of corruption and dysfunction at the uppermost levels of New Jersey's largest school system had adversely affected students' academic achievement. Newark schools consistently rated below state and national averages.

Though the process was painful, state intervention facilitated reform unencumbered by patronage and the politics of status quo so prevalent in Newark. By removing these obstacles, the state attempted to wipe the slate clean so that necessary changes could be instituted swiftly. The goal was to raise levels of academic performance to competitive standards. The state commissioner of education appointed me superintendent beginning on July 1, 1995. Choosing individuals both from within Newark's organization and from the outside, I immediately assembled a team of professionals to help me implement systemic reform. Our first order of business was to develop a 5-year plan to turn around the Newark Public Schools.

NEW BEGINNINGS

The state intervention legislation permitted us to introduce important changes in the culture of the district, to focus on student achievement above all else, and to lay a foundation for future growth. By the end of the first year, the district was reorganized to redirect $26.3 million into educational programs for students. Shifting dollars from central offices to schools helped move the heart of our agenda forward: Improve student achievement by raising the quality of instruction.

Most significant among the programs introduced was universal full-day kindergarten and intensive professional development for early childhood teachers. Statistics indicated that the longer students stayed in the system, the greater their deficiencies became. We were keenly aware that reversing chronic failure required new attitudes and a new repertoire of instructional practices. Clearly, radical change was needed and we recognized that we could not do it alone.

Soon after arriving in Newark, I reached out to Bank Street College. Familiar with its expertise and accomplishments from my days as an elementary principal and later as deputy chancellor for instruction in New York City, I knew they could help us drive revolutionary thinking in Newark.

The prevailing approach to early childhood teaching in Newark was similar to the instructional approaches used throughout the district and across the grades: "ditto" sheets, seat work, "drill & kill." Absent in most early childhood classrooms was learning that could be described as "fun." Not surprisingly, the paucity of enjoyable activities was accompanied by a lack of learning success. Given the level of student performance in all grades, it was apparent that traditional teaching approaches were inadequate. We were compelled to devise a long-term solution to this situation.

Our teachers needed to learn how to engage students in learning beginning with their very first experiences in the classroom. Our target was to ensure that students were reading by third grade. Bank Street's approach fit well with our reform strategy, so we looked to them to assist us in developing sound teaching practices—ones that promoted inquiry-driven, project-based learning while fostering students' desire to learn.

The First Years in Newark

Although I fully expected my Newark experience to be a challenge, I underestimated the level of that challenge. During the first community board meetings, it became very clear that only the voices of opposition would initially be heard. Alliances of the "old guard" would fail to support reform efforts throughout my 4 years as superintendent. Sabotage was clearly imaginable. I was fighting a culture so entrenched that I encountered resistance at every level of the organization.

Operations proved to be the most resistant to change. For example, protections afforded civil service employees thwarted efforts to develop an organization that would function in support of schools: Central office organization had become accustomed to operating as a collection of self-promoting entities. For many years, unqualified personnel had been hired for many positions through patronage and nepotism. In one particular case, the district employed a blind security guard in a school. Inefficiency prevailed throughout the division: There were numerous positions for which there were no job descriptions, and once those jobs were eliminated, the system felt no discernible impact.

In our efforts to bring efficiency to the instructional side of the house, we carefully evaluated all principals and vice-principals. I was surprised by what I perceived as the "entrenched" nature of the teaching and building-level administrative staff. Many had become complacent in their jobs. Despite widespread failure, the district had continued to conduct business as usual. The system needed a jolt, and by the end of my tenure as superintendent more than half of all principals were new to their positions.

In July 1996, 600 employees were laid off. Those layoffs were traumatic, a perceptible shock to a system that had taken easy employment for granted. This was an easy issue for the vested interest groups to exploit and misrepresent to the community. Without those layoffs, our reform agenda might have been easier to introduce and more readily embraced. However, it was necessary to shift dollars to put needed resources into the classroom, a change that I was determined to implement.

The greatest impediments to reform were the various collective-bargaining units that represented teachers, administrators, and many noninstructional staff. State takeover ended the unions' ability to manipulate the system and undermined their practice of protecting jobs and defending the status quo. Unlike my experience in New York, where the unions progressively participated in discussions of student achievement, in Newark the unions were dogged in their resistance to such conversations.

I fully understood that large urban public school systems faced enormous challenges. Yet I must confess that what I found in Newark shocked me.

The physical condition of one school we visited shortly after arriving in Newark was appalling. This particular building, which housed a summer school session when I toured it, reeked of urine; the lavatories lacked running water, stall doors, and toilet tissue; stairwells were filled with graffiti; the wall of one classroom was adorned with offensive words once written in red paint but now faded—an indication that the words had been permitted to exist for a very long time. I was told that rats the size of squirrels inhabited the basement.

The general attitude toward education in Newark was an eye-opener for me. Even "good," well-intentioned members of the community revealed to me their utter lack of faith in students' ability to learn. One member of the business community publicly pledged his support but privately told me that Newark was a lost cause, that we were rearranging chairs on the deck of the Titanic.

The level of misconduct in the Newark Public Schools startled me the most. Allegedly, there were employees who had bought their jobs with money and favors. Graft and kickbacks had occurred in district business dealings. Within my first year of arriving in Newark, I requested that the state establish an independent investigative unit to weed out corruption in the district.

Fortunately, the philanthropic community rallied to publicly support the cause of reform. I was surprised by the extent to which they were willing to invest in the future of Newark. In no small way this assistance contributed to our successes.

Support and Resistance: Implementing New Beginnings

Foundation support allowed us to form a partnership with Bank Street College to implement New Beginnings in a limited number of our kindergarten classrooms. We encountered a typical reaction to change and met with initial resistance to the Bank Street project. Many factors contributed to this resistance: From within the Newark Public Schools the takeover was still very much suspect; information was not properly disseminated; and the district's director of early childhood education was resigning. (Although she had voluntarily resigned her position, supporters viewed the partnership with Bank Street as a criticism of her and the programs she had implemented.)

Poor communication had the greatest impact on generating resistance to the program. Teachers who were chosen to participate in New

Beginnings, for example, were unaware of what they had been asked to do. They soon learned that project training would occur during the summer, a practice out of the ordinary and not readily embraced in Newark. Resistance also came from principals, who at first were only minimally involved. With time and expansion, participation became more democratic. Support networks were devised to help teachers and principals understand the goals and practices advocated by New Beginnings.

Gradually, acceptance of New Beginnings increased among teachers, students, and parents. As time went on, and assistant superintendents became more knowledgeable, the project was consolidated within specific schools in each School Leadership Team. The program was expanded horizontally and vertically, maximizing effectiveness and impact on the system.

LESSONS LEARNED

The state takeover legislation permitted us to aggressively institute a strategic plan for reform. But it was silent on an issue that is crucial to raising the level of student performance: the expeditious removal of nonperforming staff. The most significant obstacles standing in the way of reform are tenure laws, civil service regulations, and existing labor agreements. State legislation also failed to address issues of governance, leadership, and return to local control.

There was no clear rationale for having 15 members on the advisory board that replaced the 9-member school board. The law called for the commissioner of education to appoint 13 advisory board members, and the Newark City Council to appoint 2. It was clear from our board meetings, especially in those first 2 years, that the legislation should have prohibited former board members from serving on the advisory board. The board members appointed by the city council were the most disruptive members and prevented others from functioning.

However, it is important to consider whether the election of nine people is the true watermark of return to local control. We must be specific about what local control is and is not. In fact, instead of a "return" to anything, it would be more accurate to speak of a revival of democracy and community involvement in the school district. What existed in the district, prior to state operation, was anything but democratic. Control lay in a few powerful hands. Only a fraction of the eligible voters in Newark bothered to vote in school board elections. How could anyone want to return to that state of affairs?

I must also be frank about the community ambivalence toward school reform. State operation created a great deal of animosity and forced many people to take sides. The grass-roots community was not prepared for change, even those who were fed up with the old way of doing things. The school system had long reinforced underachievement by offering alarmingly generous compensation for district jobs while requiring only minimal levels of education. Generations of Newark families had come to depend on the district for gainful employment. Once again, the schools were expected to do it all, and the students ultimately suffered the consequences.

Another factor that undermined support for reform was the lack of closure on the past. There is a real connection between corruption and low-performing school systems. But the legislation is tentative when it should be definitive about why state operation is necessary. There was no swift follow-up via the criminal justice system to address the fact that there had indeed been great wrongdoing in the Newark Public Schools, nor was blame placed where it belonged for the harsh price paid in the classroom.

In the politically charged atmosphere of Newark, meaningful change must occur one school at a time by ensuring that all of the necessary elements, including good leadership and appropriate staff development, are in place. Because true reform must begin from within, buy-in is necessary to institutionalize change.

Together with my team, I was able to bring much needed stability to the district, halting the downward spiral over the course of my tenure. But years of neglect cannot be erased or mitigated overnight. Long-term change demands leadership that can focus on students and resist the interference of state and local politics. Such interference never has anything to do with the best interest of children but everything to do with the interests of adults.

The original New Beginnings students, now third graders, took state exams for the first time during the 1999–2000 school year. Our constituencies will use their performance on that test to evaluate the partnership between Bank Street College and the Newark Public Schools. However, regardless of how we choose to measure the success of this reform initiative, at the very least, our littlest students will have enjoyed their first formal educational experience. And the magnitude of that experience may be immeasurable.

6

Interview with Marion Bolden, Superintendent, The Newark Public Schools

INTERVIEW BY CAROL LIPPMAN

Marion Bolden is currently the superintendent of the Newark Public Schools. Like Lillian Burke, she is also a product of that system. She began her professional life as a classroom teacher in Newark, eventually becoming director of the Office of Mathematics and associate superintendent for teaching and learning. Assuming the superintendency upon the departure of Beverly Hall for Atlanta in 1999, Bolden has had the advantage of being an insider with a thorough understanding of the district. In this interview she candidly reflects on the current state of the schools and projects a vision for their future.

CAROL: You have a long history in Newark and a unique perspective on the school system. Looking back, I am wondering what are the most important changes you have seen over the years.

MARION: If you're asking me to go all the way back to my experiences as a student, then that span is almost 50 years. At the time I was a student I was afforded a quality education. I even received a full scholarship for undergraduate college and another, through the Thistle program funded by the Victoria Foundation, to pursue graduate work. I felt that, for the most part, the teachers were caring people. When I graduated from high school in 1964, a change in the demographics had caused a decline in the numbers of honors classes. For the most part, however, I would say that Newark was still a good place to go to school.

CAROL: Did you start teaching in Newark immediately after graduating from college?

MARION: Yes.

CAROL: And that was shortly after the 1967 riots. What was it like?

Marion: I started at Barringer High School in 1968. The school was predominantly Italian-American then. I had good classes. Even in my general math classes, most of the youngsters were not so far behind that I had to spend much time remediating. Up until I left that school, I had youngsters who were very accomplished. The teachers had high standards, held kids to certain expectations, and for the most part students performed. However, things started to decline once the exodus of middle-class families began after the riots. Some of the new teachers were not well trained. Teachers could get certified without being fully credentialed. Often they came into the system as substitute interims for a period of 2 or 3 years. Because the district was trying to quickly right the racial imbalance, it accepted teachers that perhaps I would not have accepted. Low salaries also contributed to the difficulty of recruiting excellent teachers.

It was almost immediately after the riots that there was a mass exodus of older teachers, and new, younger teachers, were apprehensive about coming into the district. There were, however, supports for the new teachers. I don't think that there have been the kinds of supports for new teachers that we had years ago. I am committed to reestablishing them. It is hard to teach in an urban district because youngsters sometimes come to school hungry and tired. They live in a world that is very different from the world of suburbia.

People coming into the district in the last 6 or 7 years find the schools old but clean. They find supplies, almost in abundance. There are certainly going to be situations where for one reason or another there is a shortage of something. Because we work cooperatively and one school can get supplies from another, there is less likelihood of this happening.

The potential, right now for Newark, is unbelievable. It's huge, no question. I mean, you just need to drive into the city to see it. Where one of my staff who is fairly new to the district says that she senses despair, I sense just the opposite. I sense hope and optimism for the first time in many years.

I feel that the community is now more aware of what needs to be done in the district, and is willing to help. I do not know that people are going to be patient forever. There needs to be some tangible evidence that things are getting better. But corporate America, corporate Newark—let me not say corporate America—does have a belief that we can turn things around. For example, Prudential Life Insurance, Lucent Technologies, and PSE&G have become some of our largest corporate supporters. If nothing else, it inspires me to know that the district has the support of teachers in the classrooms and from the corporate community.

It's the early childhood programs that are going to make a big difference. I do not think that we have focused enough on the kindergartens. In the past, if the kids were there and having fun, then that was wonderful. Now, because there is a state assessment that requires youngsters to demonstrate what they can do, people are more attentive to what goes on in early childhood classes. However, it should have always been that way.

CAROL: How long have you been in the district?

MARION: I taught mathematics at Barringer High School for 14 years. After teaching, I became the department chair at Arts High School. Then I was the director of mathematics for the district for 6 years. Eventually I was appointed associate superintendent for teaching and learning, and during that time Dr. Hall asked me to take on the job of assistant superintendent of the secondary schools. Now that I am superintendent of schools, it's fortunate that I've had experience in other areas, especially as associate superintendent of teaching and learning. I found myself in many different venues, and I was forced to develop a more global understanding of what needs to be done.

Because I was the one responsible for pre-K to 12 curriculum development, it also became evident that I would have to determine the effectiveness of all instructional initiatives in the district, including the early childhood programs. I decided that the best way to learn about good instruction was to see for myself. When I visited early childhood classrooms with Dr. Jan Stewart, an early childhood professor at Caldwell College, I recognized quality instruction without needing to be told. These firsthand observations made it apparent, even through the eyes of a mathematics director, that there were significant differences in the methodologies being used in our early childhood classes. I soon discovered that many of the exemplary, highly interactive classes were part of Bank Street's Project New Beginnings. As required in the Newark Curriculum Guides, I found learning centers and multicultural, thematic units that supported the goals and objectives of the New Jersey Core Curriculum Standards. I also observed a social environment that encouraged a sense of community while valuing each individual, whether child, teacher, aide, or administrator. Good teaching is good teaching no matter what the grade level or subject matter.

CAROL: Interviewing Cathy McFarland of the Victoria Foundation and Lillian Burke, principal of Clinton Avenue Elementary School, I was struck by how they spoke about the decline of Newark. Lillian talks about the impact of the riots and Cathy dates the decline of the city to the "arson for profit" in preceding years. What do you see as the impact on the school system of the riots, the arson, and resulting homeless population?

MARION: It all had a great impact and Cathy is probably right in terms of the arson predating the riots. There was something that created the riots—hope was missing and despair was pervasive. In terms of my own perspective, you have to remember that during the riots I was a senior in college just preparing to enter the educational scene.

I was living in the city at the time, but I was not as aware as I should have been of what was going on in the schools. Certainly I have read the history and know about the problems. As a high school youngster, I saw some inequities. And I saw more when I got out of school.

Retrospectively, I understand that at South Side High School I was not afforded as good a situation as students in other neighborhood schools in terms of the course offerings. But I was not so disadvantaged that I wasn't able to do well. It's just that in certain cases there were lower expectations and in some cases there were no expectations for excellence at all. My awareness really began when I was a college student. Looking back, I recognize that there were advantages that I did not have. But I didn't know that I was poor until I got out into the larger world. I was never hungry or without the essentials. I was a young African-American woman, and that prevented me from having some of the enrichment that others had at that time.

The period after the riots was hard. Yes, as the ethnicity in the district changed, so did the quality of education. That is apparent to any novice who looks at the record. Given where we are now, it would be difficult to go back there again, but not impossible. It is different because we are an urban district and people no longer make mistakes about how hard they must work when they come here.

They know what it is that they will find and we know the kind of teacher we must recruit.

There are, unfortunately, people who want an easier job. Perhaps that's unfair to say. But there are some people who are not able to deal with rough situations out of choice or temperament. Every situation in Newark is not a hard one. Once you get your class, establish respect, and engage your students, you find that they are like students anywhere. Most often, when a teacher has discipline problems it is because she is not doing what she needs to do to engage the kids. Our kids are products of their environment. Many of our kids do not get the nurturing that they need at home. In some cases, school is the only place they look forward to going.

The kind of teachers we need know what to teach, how to model good character, and when to show their love to the students. We can teach them the pedagogy. There are some who struggle with that. Overall, when I look at the new teachers we hired this year, I am pleased. They are enthused. They know that we are a struggling school district; we are about to be reborn. I try to guarantee that the supports that they need will be there. We have been aggressive in offering individual mentoring and $500 incentives for new teachers just to show them that somebody does care. More than just a few somebodies—a whole school district cares. That's what they have to believe. They have to believe in the system. And that is the work that I have yet to do.

CAROL: You have created a very positive climate, a climate of hope. That's what you are really talking about. Yet the despair you are trying to undo has such a long history.

MARION: My kids don't think there is a Brass Ring. If the teachers believe, then that's what they will convey to the kids. There are some things that we have to do as a district to give them tangible evidence that change is happening. When I go to a football game, I want to see a band presence out there on the field. I want to see cheerleaders. I brought the band directors down to my office to communicate my expectations. If you are telling me that you need uniforms, then I will find someone to help pay for them. We had 11 students in the band last year at West Side High School and now we have 115. You can't tell me that with the right personnel you can't do it. We have hired new young teachers who come with energy and vision and passion. If you have that, yes we can move mountains. That's what we are attempting to do.

At the same time we have to look at the quality of instruction. So I want a feel-good situation, but I also want evidence of student achievement. When I started 30 years ago, teachers had certain expectations about the summer off, orderly classrooms, and no big issues. Now teachers say, if I come to Newark, I know that I have to be a nurturing, caring teacher. I want to do that for youngsters who are underprivileged. That's the kind of teacher I want.

CAROL: How has this school year, 2000–2001, begun?

MARION: The convocation that we had with the teachers had a larger impact than I had hoped. We talked about helping new teachers and stressed that they weren't out there by themselves. When I visited schools the week after, some of the veteran teachers wanted me to come into their class, but they also wanted to tell me what they were doing for one of the new teachers. The teachers were highly motivated and I was motivated because the teachers left feeling uplifted. We also talked to them about the district, our plans, and our vision. We described what this administration was all about and emphasized that we needed their help to achieve our goals. We can't do it without them.

CAROL: It sounds like a good beginning.

MARION: I say if we don't do it now, I don't know when there is going to be another window to get it right. It is also a matter of mutual respect, because if you are fearful and intimidated, you want to leave the school building at 2:30. I'm not talking about respect without accountability. My staff gets stressed. But I am not asking them to do what they can't do. If you can't do it, I have to make changes, not because I am mean-spirited but because—who is this about? Kids! And if you can't deliver, you better find a job doing something else. In the end, the history of this city will tell us, once again, we can't fail our kids. Education is for them! They have to be able to reach that Brass Ring.

PART II

TEACHING AND LEARNING

T HE LITERATURE on school change suggests that even in wealthy, innovative districts filled with high-achieving students, staff development projects may require between 3 and 5 years to take hold (Anyon, 1994). To this caution about time, we add a further caution about scale. In its 3rd year, the project was scattered in 19 different sites across Newark, and, although the 4th year saw a consolidation into 10 schools, at any one time staff developers were working in well over 100 pre-K to third-grade classrooms. Michael Fullan (1982) comments on the difficulties of promoting change in large school districts:

> If change attempts are to be successful, individuals and groups must find meaning concerning *what* should change as well as *how* to go about it. Yet it is exceedingly difficult to resolve the problem of meaning when large numbers of people are involved. (p. ix)

During the first 2 years of the project, many teachers made significant changes in their pedagogy across the curriculum. Staff developers worked with the teachers to whom they were assigned to develop goals in keeping with their personal professional agenda, be it classroom management skills, science curriculum, or math activities. Some teachers preferred that Bank Streeters only observe or provide special curriculum materials, whereas others invited them to conduct model lessons, assist with teacher-led activities, and help out with difficult children. Although New Beginnings staff developers shared a common set of philosophic principles, the *what* and *how* of the change process was tailored to meet the needs of individual teachers.

Toward the end of the 2nd and throughout the 3rd year of the project, teachers and staff developers joined together to familiarize themselves with the new literacy programs—Children's Literacy Initiative (CLI), Diagnostic Reading Assessment (DRA), Guided

Reading—being introduced by the district. These literacy initiatives finally functioned as the common ground on which teachers and staff developers were able to navigate as equals with full district approval.

Most staff development programs have implicit within them a deficit model of existing teaching. After all, why else would "experts" be retained by a school if not to fix something that was broken? With the focus on literacy, New Beginnings engaged in program building more than program critique. Needless to say, this could not have occurred without the existence of the trust and communication skills built in the preceding 2 years. Nor could it have occurred without the project's outreach to the new initiatives. Staff developers worked side by side with teachers to integrate the new reading program into the structures—interest centers, small-group and individual instruction, sustained work periods—originally developed to support a more diversified curriculum. The positive impact of this approach was evidenced by the marked decrease in teacher references to the "two masters" theme heard so frequently during the first years. In its place was a greater sense of shared purpose. Student outcomes benefited as well, for at the end of 3 years in New Beginnings classrooms, students scored significantly higher than did their non–New Beginnings peers on all components of the Stanford 9 achievement test (Kopacsi & Onsongo, 1999; see Appendix).

Although the urgency of the literacy focus placed subjects like social studies and art temporarily on the back burner, it did not distract from the primary New Beginnings goal of creating early childhood classrooms in which "children are actively and wholly engaged—cognitively, socially, emotionally and physically—in the process of learning" (Project New Beginnings, 2000). Building on trends begun in the first years of the project, New Beginnings classrooms offered a range of structures in which teaching–learning might occur, encouraged student independence, and provided many opportunities for students to learn from each other (Schwartz, Silin, & Miserendino, 1999; Silin & Schwartz, 2000). Where once teachers made clear distinctions between New Beginnings–inspired curriculum and Newark Public School mandates, now it is increasingly difficult to tell them apart.

Research indicates that New Beginnings classrooms are relaxed, interactive environments in which students are free to move around, make choices about how and when they complete tasks, and talk with each other about the work at hand (Schwartz & Silin, 2002). The sheer volume of student talk contributes to a workshoplike atmosphere as well as to the development of linguistic skills. We can also hypothesize that the planning, consulting, and negotiating among the children contributes to the sense of responsibility that they exercise for their own learning and behavior. It undoubtedly contributes to the development of organizational skills and an increased repertoire of learning strategies. In contrast to the non–New Beginnings classrooms, project classrooms promote and sustain a more productive peer culture that enhances and diversifies learning opportunities.

For their part, New Beginnings teachers are more responsive than their non–New Beginnings peers to the interests and individual needs of their students. Not only are New Beginnings teachers accepting of personal stories shared by students, but many have learned to employ a more open-ended questioning style that facilitates critical thinking. Working with flexibly structured small groups and with individuals, project teachers spend more time observing and listening to their students before responding to their queries. New Beginnings teachers are curious about *how* children think as well as *what* they think, the process as well as the product of their intellectual labors.

The essays in Part II, Teaching and Learning, depict some of the changes that have occurred in Newark Public School classrooms. Betsy Blachly and Sandra Heintz, Lenore Furman and Kathleen Hayes, two teacher–staff developer pairs, testify to what can happen when educators find a shared passion, in the first instance music and in the second social studies. Nancy Balaban, a staff developer, talks about helping to create a democratic community in the classroom of a teacher for whom everything about New Beginnings was truly new. In contrast, Joan Bojsza, a seasoned early childhood teacher, identifies her work with New Beginnings as a homecoming, a return to ways of teaching that she had abandoned under pressure of mandates, assessments, and bureaucratic red tape. Finally, retelling children's stories from a second-grade classroom, Lesley Koplow, coordinator of the New Beginnings mental health project, explores the processes through which children make sense of social identities. Together, these essays offer insight into the thinking of New Beginnings teachers and the experiences of their students.

7

This Train Is Crossing the River

BETSY BLACHLY AND SANDRA HEINTZ

Betsy Blachly teaches at the Bank Street School for Children and is a staff developer for Project New Beginnings. Sandy Heintz, formerly a classroom teacher, is a resource teacher coordinator in the Newark Public Schools. In this essay, the authors take turns describing their work together over a 2-year period and the significant changes it brought about in Sandy's classroom. Here is Betsy, a skillful staff developer in action, knowing when to push and when to hold back, how to seize serendipitous moments and how to construct others as needed. Here too is Sandy, an experienced and motivated teacher taking advantage of every staff development opportunity to enhance and enrich her curriculum.

Betsy: An Itinerant Song Leader

BETSY: Guess what I like to do?

CHILDREN: Play that! Play. . . . Sing! Play guitar?

BETSY: Yes, I like to play my guitar and sing. (pause) But, I didn't come to sing by myself. There's something else I really like to do. Can you guess?

CHILDREN: Sing. Sing with kids? With me? With all the kids!!!

BETSY: You're right. I like to play and sing with all the kids when I visit your school. I also like to sing with teachers. Your school asked me here today to sing together with you. I'm going to sing some songs that you know, like "Old MacDonald," and some songs that you don't know. I always like to start with this song written by Ella

Jenkins about singing a song. I'm going to listen to you sing along with me as soon as you figure out the words.

"You sing a song, and I'll sing a song."

BETSY: Hey, wow, that sounds terrific! Did you hear the sound of everyone singing together? Let's do it again.

"You sing a song and I'll sing a song."

What sounds can we all make together with our bodies? I noticed that some of you were clapping already. Who wants to make up another sound?

I am a seasoned itinerant song leader in schools, and the above words are part of my opener. I always start with this song when I first meet children, whether in Newark, with the Project New Beginnings, or in the public schools in Manhattan, the Bronx, Brooklyn, or Jersey City.

Each time I sing together with children and their teachers, the experience in that room, and in that school, is unique. This is because singing happens in time, and it is a social activity. You can't plan what happens when voices, faces, bodies, harmony, songs, and individual associations get together.

Within the safety net of the song, everybody claps, claps-taps, clicks tongues, speeds up, slows down, stops suddenly, guffaws, jumps, dances in a small circle, moos, oinks, and twinkles. They sing with gusto when told "that's a beautiful sound," and, if they yell, I tell them that "singing is not yelling." Everybody laughs, gets silly, stops getting silly, listens, tries to rhyme, calls out songs to sing, watches each other, and, in the end, sings bye-bye.

Then I move into the next classroom and I encounter another mood. All these interactions and exchanges happen again, but the children, the teachers, the music, and I bond in a different way. I never tire of meeting these children in the context of singing.

Sandy: A Kindergarten Teacher

I became part of Project New Beginnings during the summer of 1996. Dr. Carol Lippman and her crew from Bank Street College met with 16 kindergarten teachers, myself included, that summer. In the fall a staff developer came to our rooms each week, and we were also given many opportunities to visit the Bank Street School for Children. There, I first saw Betsy Blachly in action.

During that first visit to the Bank Street School for Children, I observed the weekly Wednesday morning assembly, where 115 children in the lower school sing, together with their teachers. Parents are invited too. Watching them sitting on the floor in the music room, joining in with as much gusto as their children, I could feel that the music provided a way for everyone to connect. For a brief moment, I tried to envision this communal joy in my school. I sang along, and tried hard to commit words and melodies to memory. My colleague Lenore Furman was there with me, and later she and I were able to help each other recall what we heard.

The second time I observed at the School for Children, Betsy was singing in a 5/6 classroom. The children wanted to sing the song with the verses they had written. As Betsy pulled out a chart with the children's words, I saw immediately that music could be a powerful literacy learning tool.

The time I spent observing Betsy as a music teacher couldn't have added up to more than 40 or 45 minutes. But the impact was enormous, and the possibilities were becoming evident . . . but not yet within my grasp.

Betsy in the Lobby

At Bank Street, a good place to talk is right by the front door. Usually, you are leaving or coming in, and there is someone trying to do the same. When I saw Carol Lippman by the front door, I have to admit I cornered her. I had heard the announcement about a program in Newark called New Beginnings and that she was in charge. I introduced myself and told her why I thought music, specifically singing, can be a strong part of community development. We scheduled an appointment. While talking to Carol in the lobby, I could already hear in my head that amazing sound of children's voices singing together in the classroom.

Sandy in her Classroom

Singing together in the classroom was not exactly foreign to me. As a teacher who came to the primary grades by way of preschool and Head Start classrooms, I knew that music could be used to transition children smoothly from one activity to another. I was very aware of the inherent joy in group singing, yet I still viewed music as something frivolous in a primary classroom. Singing was not seen as an end in itself, with purposes of its own, but merely as a vehicle to lead us to something of "real importance." For example, I'd often use a song to get the children's attention, or the song would be a reward for a job well done.

New Beginnings was giving me license to explore new ideas and ways of teaching. I wanted music to become a vehicle for both learning and community building and to help children feel confident and competent. With the support of New Beginnings, I imagined that I might have the freedom to try this out. Then my staff developer told me that Betsy was available to visit each New Beginnings classroom once during the year. With Betsy's help, I thought I might be able to make this nebulous vision of what music can be for children a reality. I would make the best of it, even if she was a "one shot deal."

Betsy Reflects

In my work as an itinerant music teacher I have experienced frustration with "one shot deals." Sometimes I get a chance to talk to teachers after a visit, and they tell me that they observed some surprising moments: A child who is quiet becomes talkative; another child becomes a leader, because she has learned the words right away; one child remembers a color that he didn't know an hour ago. A teacher will ask me how a song goes, or did I know such and such a song from her or his childhood? Though these are significant conversations, this is my only visit; there will not be a follow-up. It makes me feel that even lovely moments are "squeezed in." This adds to my feeling of frustration. Will I ever think, "My work's done"?

Singing is important because songs take you to a place that speaking words can't get to. As each "me" joins in, the sound instantly becomes "us," displacing isolation with welcoming inclusion. Songs are my materials, and as a music educator I am intrigued by the transformations that children naturally experience. However, as a music staff developer my focus is on the teachers. My job is to provide modeling, encouragement, and repertoire for potential use in their classroom. Although teachers may be curious, they are often scared and nervous; usually they are worried about not being "good enough." Sometimes I wish I could break the ice with a group of teachers by asking, "Do any of you have a guitar at home in your closet?"

Sandy: Betsy's First Visit

For years prior to Betsy's first visit, I had stored away a once-used guitar in a rarely opened closet in my house. I had purchased the guitar thinking, "This would be a great instrument to play with children." When Betsy entered my room with her guitar in hand, instantaneously all eyes were focused on her and the instrument. I remember wondering, "Now where did I stash that guitar?"

Betsy sang Merle Gettrell's "Hold the Dream," a song about Martin Luther King that I knew but had always thought too wordy for young children. It was January, and the children had read several books about Dr. King. Betsy asked, "What do you know about Martin Luther King?" A child said, "He had a father who was a preacher." Another child said, "He was shot by a bad man." Those sentences became the words of the verse. The children were transformed into lyricists.

"You could learn to play an instrument," Betsy said to me during that first visit. I didn't even mention the guitar that sat untouched in my house. "I doubt it. I have no ability in that area." Certainly I saw how focused the children became when the guitar accompanied their singing, and certainly I wanted to play an instrument. I simply thought that learning to do this was one trick this old dog couldn't master.

Even without guitar accompaniment, the children and I had been making joyful music together that year. Singing was given a place of importance, with a specific time set aside each day. Children wrote their own words to songs and added their own verses to old songs. I sent words home so that parents could sing songs from the classroom with their children, and parents were encouraged to come in with their own well-loved songs for us to learn. We developed group favorites, which gave us a collective identity and helped us to develop a sense of community. My guitar still sat unplayed.

Betsy: 1998 Summer Institute

This summer I was scheduled to spend 3 days at Clinton Avenue Elementary School in the space of 2 weeks. Three days was consistency. I could actually start a connection with some children or a teacher, and experience the gratification of a follow-up.

I learned the first morning that Sandy was one of the summer institute teachers. Wasn't Sandy Heintz the woman who had a cheerful demeanor, who was comfortable singing, and whose children wrote the verses to "Hold the Dream" last January?

When I entered her classroom, Sandy and I smiled at each other. To my enormous pleasure, there were several children who, remembering my visit to Clinton in the winter, exclaimed, "OOooooo, let's sing the one about the train." I said, "Absolutely, we will definitely sing 'This Train,' but first let's do that song about singing a song."

I have come to respect and rely on the African-American traditional song "This Train" because it is a magnet for children's words.

"This train is bound for glory, this train is bound for glory.
This train is bound for glory. Children, get on board."

Whenever I ask, "Where is your train going?" or "Who was on the train with you?" many hands go up instantly. Sometimes as many as 15 children want to say their idea. Meanwhile, the simple two-chord structure and the middle vocal range of the melody allow for easy singing. The second chord is the flat VII, which supports the modal melody, which in turn urges you to join the song. "This Train" is definitely an old friend.

Sandy: Watching Betsy

I remember watching closely as Betsy moved her fingers to change chords. When I glanced up from her fingers, it was obvious that Betsy had observed my interest. "Do you want to learn to play a chord?" she asked me. I had the desire, but I felt I lacked the aptitude. I showed her my rather short fingers in an effort to discourage her. She flashed me her even smaller ones! I surrendered when she said, "Shall we meet at lunch?"

Betsy: Watching Sandy

That day in July, I observed Sandy looking at my chord hand. Was she figuring out that there were only two chords in the entire song? At the end of the song, I murmured, "This is a pretty easy song to play." I wanted her to know that I noticed her noticing. When the classes' music time was over, I asked as casually as possible if she wanted to learn to play a chord.

Sandy: The Lunchtime Lesson

We were joined by my 10-year-old daughter Kate and Taleah, the daughter of a New Beginnings staff developer. I was feeling a bit insecure about attempting to play guitar, but Betsy encouraged me. "You have wonderful musical instincts," she told me. "You can do this." After an hour, she had me playing an E minor and a D chord and strumming less awkwardly.

I finally admitted to her that I had a guitar hidden away. She promised to give me a lesson on Thursday, if I'd bring along my guitar. Feeling some measure of confidence at this point, I agreed to dig it out of its hiding place. Kate and Taleah were caught up in the moment. "Let's bring our flute and violin on Thursday, too." Thursday was going to be a lovely, musical day.

Betsy: The Lunchtime Lesson

Thursday *was* a lovely, musical day! There was Sandy, with her guitar that she had secretly bought years ago, her daughter Kate, the flute player, and Taleah, the violin player. I tuned the guitar and complimented its shape. Sandy told me all about it. (Guitars are such friendly instruments and people always talk about them in glowing terms, especially after a long separation.) We reviewed what she had tried on Tuesday. Time passed quickly, and I gave her the music "lead sheets" to support her learning.

Sandy was an excellent student. She didn't spend too much time complaining about the pain or the klutzy feeling in her fingers. Inside, I was feeling excited for her. She had already discovered the context for singing in her classroom. Now including the guitar would spark her personal enjoyment, while the children, accompanied harmonically as well as melodically, would be witness to the doubts and joys of the learning process.

There was another wrinkle that was catching my well-trained eye: Kate was watching me teach Sandy just as intently as Sandy had been watching me on Tuesday. Aha, I thought to myself, another person in this family who is a quick study.

Sandy: The Bank Street Lesson

It was clear that Betsy was not going to allow me to warehouse the guitar back in the closet once the summer institute had ended. At Betsy's suggestion, Carol Lippman agreed to fund one guitar lesson for me later that summer. We were to meet across the river at Bank Street College. My daughter Kate asked to come along. Impulsively, we purchased a ¾ guitar on the way to the train station. We arrived in New York City, carrying our two guitars.

Betsy: The Bank Street Lesson

Sandy walked into the music room—with Kate and two guitars! It was déjà vu: tuning the guitar, hearing the story about getting Kate's guitar, tuning hers, and commenting on it. They were both ready for work.

Now the bar had been raised: Sandy was coming into New York City for a lesson with me that was not "squeezed in" and was subsidized by New Beginnings. It was a generous move for the project to foster musical curiosity in an already enthusiastic teacher. To me, of course, it was musical staff development at its best.

Thirty minutes later the "A7 moment" had arrived. Rounding this small guitar corner brings at least 10 songs into the early childhood song repertoire.

There was a definite buzz in the room now, and I decided to stretch the envelope. Knowing that I might not see Sandy again, I said, "OK, one more chord. It's called G. It opens the door to about 450 more songs, including the blues and early rock 'n roll." I showed the mother–daughter team the G chord. There were the usual howls of pain. When Sandy said, "I'll never learn G," I smiled.

Sandy: A First-Grade Teacher, Fall 1998

Finally my fingers managed to learn G. I found the discipline to practice what Betsy had taught me. Now I can play songs with three chords.

Following the summer institute and my one glorious day of guitar instruction, I started teaching first grade at Abington Avenue School that September. Although I was naturally apprehensive about changing schools and grade levels, I was thrilled to be teaching at the same school with Lenore Furman, a teacher who was part of New Beginnings' first cohort too. She was someone I had grown to admire. We had previously collaborated when our students became pen pals, so I approached Lenore about the possibility of having our group sing together throughout the year. She eagerly agreed to meet monthly for "community sings."

Despite my original concern with the change in schools and grade levels, it seemed to me that we were moving along swimmingly.

Then I hit a speed bump.

Newark can be a difficult city in which to teach. I had always tried to balance what was required by the district with what I knew about how children learn and what my heart tells me is right. This system had worked well for me until one morning during my first year at Abington when the vice-principal called me into her office.

I entered the office with a feeling of dread that would soon be confirmed; she informed me that a parent had complained that I wasn't "teaching" reading. She wouldn't tell me the name of the parent, so I was unable to speak directly to the parent about specific concerns. I did tell the vice-principal how balanced literacy works in my room. I explained how I use our song charts, along with big books and other charts, for shared reading. I told her how we use songs to analyze text. I spoke to her about the guided reading and writing programs, and showed her evidence of students' progress. The vice-principal asked a resource teacher from the early childhood department to visit my classroom during the year and to offer me whatever guidance and staff development she felt was necessary. All of this left me feeling apprehensive, protective, and insecure. I thought I had a good program. I thought we were learning well together and coming together as a group. I couldn't believe that my perception might be so off base.

The resource teacher from the district office came on many occasions to observe my practice. She was appreciative of the joy in our classroom and pleased with the democratic community we had established. What's more, she saw the value in everything that we did, from journal writing in the morning until our final meeting in the afternoon. She recognized that songs and song charts could be used to teach literacy as many might use poetry. She recognized immediately the benefits of coming together in song and the evidence of communal delight. She became confident in my abilities as a teacher, and with time, so did my school administration.

Betsy: Visit to Abington, December 1999

I arranged to come on a Friday, and to my delight I learned that Friday was the day that Sandy Heintz's and Lenore Furman's classes got together to—guess what—sing! Up until then, I had not known that Sandy had transferred to Abington, nor did I know that she and Lenore were holding "community sings." Of course, it made complete sense that Sandy would have gotten such an event together.

Watching this simple sharing confirmed my belief that there is no substitute for live music. Songs are very personal to children, because they attach their own meanings to each song. Children often say, "I have that song." When they say, "I have that song" I believe that they actually do *have* that song, inside themselves; they actually feel it in some physical way.

I stayed second fiddle to Sandy. She was doing great, the children from the two classrooms had bonded, and the sound in the room that day was lovely. Inside I felt, "My work's done."

Sandy: Spring 1999

During the spring of 1999, Lenore and I expanded our program by inviting parents to join us in our "community sings." We typed lyrics to the songs we sang together and photocopied them for the families to share at home. Our two rooms hosted a "Bedtime Story" event. The children were invited to come to school in the early evening wearing their pajamas for bedtime stories, snacks they had made during the school day, and, of course, bedtime songs. The parents were able to watch and participate as their children read and created words to songs, and they were able to form a link with their children's entire class through music.

Betsy: Thinking About Sandy

When I received the invitation to submit a proposal for this book, I instantly knew whom to call. Sandy and I had both crossed the Hudson and had made a link through singing. I regarded her highly as a sensitive, motivated, and devoted teacher who was naturally respectful of children. In addition, she had a close relationship to her own personal music-making. She was compelled to search for musical common ground at her own level of proficiency. Her expertise was not the point. It was the communication and connection that she sought, for herself as well as for the children.

Sandy and I were lucky to have met each other. The timing was exquisite. But what about other "Sandys" in the Newark schools? I'll never have the opportunity to watch them watch me with that "if only I could do that" look. These teachers share Sandy's hidden dream to pursue whatever instrument (or voice) that is hidden in their "closet." My years of experience had allowed me to feel confident about giving Sandy that first "nudge." Years ago, I would not have been so certain.

It is the children and teachers whom I have been singing with in various public schools who taught me that certainty. To paraphrase a traditional song, there are many "lights" that are ready to "shine" in schools like Newark's, but the shining must be for longer than the duration of the singing, if social justice is the goal.

Sandy Reflects

I have come to respect the powerful force of song in the classroom. Each year, the children seem to make one song their own, to develop an "our song," if you will. Everyone feels good when singing with others; song is the great unifier. Not everyone can read with fluency, not everyone can compute, not everyone can produce representational art, but everyone can sing along with the group, in his or her own way.

I can set the tone in my room through my choice of song. I can make the group release energy by singing "Jump Jim Joe" or "Chicka Boom." Everyone will look at each other meaningfully when we sing "What a Wonderful World." Everyone will quiet down and become reflective when we sing "Listen to the Water." The feelings are there inside the children; the songs bring them out.

I have been able to share some of my personal life through music. A favorite song in book form is "A, You're Adorable." The children are particularly fond of this book and song because they know it is one my father frequently sang to me as a child. They have also come to know songs that were passed down to me by my grandmother. During parents' "interviews" in our classroom, we ask them to share songs from their childhood or in their native language.

Betsy: Meeting Sandy in Newark, May 2000

When Sandy and I went down the hall to her classroom, two third-grade girls, waiting to be picked up after school, asked if they could "come see Ms. Heintz's guitar." I figured that this was not the first time.

There was Sandy's guitar, in its guitar stand, in the meeting area. One of the girls picked it up and sat down. She already knew E minor and she began to sing "This Train." She asked about the other chord; she found it pretty easily. I asked her if she wanted to play on the smaller guitar that I had brought along as a donation to the school from New Beginnings. She agreed. She practiced there for 15 minutes, and then asked Ms. Heintz if she could show her mother. In came her mother. More pride, more singing voices. When they left, I wondered aloud if Sandy and I could talk now without paying attention to the other child. Sandy explained that this girl often came to her room to look around, and was comfortable being independent.

However, we were in for a surprise. When she said, "Ms. Betsy, may I try the guitar?" I said, "Of course." She said, "But I only have four fingers." I said, "That shouldn't be a problem." I hadn't even noticed her hands, but her right hand had three fingers and a thumb. I said, "Hold the guitar this way." I watched as her right hand naturally took an almost strumming position. Sandy figured out later that she had been watching the other girl for all these months. When she saw the smaller guitar, she could not resist trying it.

She instantly figured out how to play the E minor chord and needed only a little help with the D chord. More "This Train." Soon the intercom announced that she was to come to the front desk to be picked up. We both said, "Bring your mom down to see." It was her big brother who came to watch her singing and changing chords and making a fine sound come out of the guitar with her three fingers. It was an unforgettable magic music moment.

8

Creating a Caring, Democratic Classroom Community for and with Young Children

NANCY BALABAN

Nancy Balaban is a member of the Bank Street Graduate Faculty with many years of experience as a staff developer. In this essay she describes her work with a teacher, Ellen, for whom absolutely everything about New Beginnings was new. She quickly assumes the challenges of creating a democratic classroom community, one in which she is no longer in front of the chalkboard all day and the children learn to solve social problems on their own. Balaban documents the children's discussions about their sometimes difficult lives as well as the ways that Ellen's thinking about her classroom evolves over time.

W ORKING WITH on-the-job early childhood teachers and paraprofessionals who are often eager for change, yet resistant and fearful of it, has been an exciting part of my teaching life. Whether the teacher is an aide in a public prekindergarten, a student teacher in a private nursery, or a head teacher in a kindergarten, the challenge for me, as supervisor/mentor, is to foster that person's growth and development. Having been well mentored myself (by having another attend carefully and "caringly" to the details of my work), I have found mentoring others to be a magnetic draw—an opportunity for "giving back." My mentoring practice has ripened over a long period of time—beginning with teaching 3- and 4-year-olds to the work I have done for the last 30 years, supervising graduate students in urban schools.

When the opportunity came to join New Beginnings, I found it irresistible. The work held not only the promise of mentoring but also the challenge of becoming involved in a school system that was no stranger to racial tensions and the concomitant struggles of teaching and learning.

One of the schools to which I was assigned had a new principal although many of the staff were long-term. My presence seemed extraneous to the new administrator, who may have been feeling very burdened, especially at this time of the state takeover. The school was orderly and relations among the teachers were generally cordial. Ellen,* the teacher with whom I worked, felt there were small ways in which unspoken feelings about race arose between her as a White person and the predominantly African-American staff.

Ellen, who had spent the prior month of June attending workshops at Bank Street, welcomed me into her kindergarten. She had been a first-grade teacher for many years and had moved to kindergarten in order to participate in New Beginnings. Because her reputation in the school was that of a good teacher, she was usually left alone to do her work—a case of benign neglect. Although she was content to be "on her own," she longed for more support and intellectual stimulation. She saw New Beginnings as an opportunity to enrich her teaching. She regarded herself as a learner and was eager to expand her knowledge of children and curriculum. Certain personal characteristics made us a good match. Since my demeanor is nonauthoritarian, she believed I would be sympathetic to her goals. In addition, we had similar backgrounds. I was much older and very experienced. I knew we had time on our side, for this was not a 1-year project.

Although I mentored other teachers in the program, none threw themselves so wholeheartedly into the process. Some made changes in form but failed to grasp the deeper meanings implicit in our staff development work. One conducted morning meetings sitting on the floor but continued to rely on authoritarian control rather than foster the children's thinking. Another provided an array of activities, such as painting, blocks, and dramatic play, but assigned children to specific areas rather than allowing them to choose. Mostly these teachers politely resisted my efforts.

---

*names are pseudonyms.

I worked with Ellen over a period of 3 years, helping her to create a caring, democratic classroom community. I have chosen to describe in detail the first year of my journey with her because it was so extraordinarily successful both from her perspective and from mine. I believe that of all the teachers I worked with, she was the most ready for change.

COMMUNITY AND COMMUNICATION IN THE CLASSROOM

In her book *Experimenting With the World: John Dewey and the Early Childhood Classroom*, Harriet Cuffaro (1995) writes that, according to John Dewey, without communication there is no community. Dewey is clear about this connection:

> There is more than a verbal tie between the words common, community, and communication. Men live in a community in virtue of the things which they have in common; and communication is the way they come to possess things in common. (Dewey, 1916/1966, p. 4)

How does an early childhood teacher create a democratic community with young children? What do teachers and young children possess in common? How and about what do they communicate? What is their shared work and what is their shared common purpose—the two basic elements that form the cornerstone of community?

These questions were very much on my mind in the years I worked with Ellen. These are not easy ideas to introduce to teachers who have been acculturated to a system in which directives come from the top down (Anyon, 1997), and in which teaching skills and taking tests have been the mainstay of the classroom. Certainly they are not easy ideas for a whole school system to accept and incorporate.

I will address these questions about creating a democratic community one at a time and explain how Ellen moved closer to forming such a community in her kindergarten.

What Do Teachers and Young Children Share in Common?

They both share a keen desire for learning. Because young children learn in their own many-faceted ways that are distinctly different from those of adults, teachers must honor, respect, and support children's unique ways of knowing. This demands a teacher's intentionality and her belief that it requires a joint effort between herself and the children to make a classroom work.

Ellen very much wanted to change her way of working with children. She was used to "keeping order" and to giving direct lessons. She was more infatuated with how she was teaching than with how the children were learning. "I wanted to be the best teacher," she told me, "I was forgetting about the kids." In this project, we were asking her to share the keeping of order with the children and to let it reside "in the shared work being done" (Dewey, 1938/1972, p. 55). Because this was a major change of direction for her, she was understandably scared. Although initially she and I spoke different philosophical and educational languages, we wanted to communicate with one another. We shared a common desire for change in her classroom. Our work together, in which she was the main decision maker and creator of change, reflected, in many essential ways, her own course with the children.

At the core of our relationship there had to be trust. Ellen had to trust that I would support and help her as she moved along a new and untried path and that I would not be critical of her efforts. The children had to trust her to see them not only as a group but as individuals. Ellen also had to trust the children to make decisions, solve problems, and make choices. This was a very tall order.

When you have seen yourself, as Ellen did, as the provider of answers, the "boss," and the decision maker, it takes great courage to move toward becoming a facilitator, a collaborator, and a community builder.

How and About What Do Teachers and Children Communicate?

Building a community requires the teacher to interact with—communicate with—children through words, activities, and materials. Not just any words, activities, and materials, but those that promote opportunities for children to work and think together.

> It is in materials and activities that lend themselves to sharing ideas, to utilizing common space and objects, to encouraging communication among participants, to generating varied functions in work, that a sense of community and shared purpose emerges and a democratic vision begins. (Cuffaro, 1995, p. 36)

Materials such as blocks, sand, water, clay, paint, and dough, which Cuffaro (1995) describes as the "texts" of early childhood education, beckon children to make their impact upon them. Ellen had never used any of these materials during her 8 years of teaching. She had no prior experience in giving children choices about which activities or materials to use. Now she had to think about and plan how the day would go and how the room would be arranged in order to facilitate children's free choices and movement. And she had to decide how she would communicate these intentions to the children.

It is within the context of choice, time, and space that children and teachers begin to create a democratic community of learners, doers, and caring individuals. Such communities do not occur spontaneously. Dewey (1938/1972) comments, "Community life does not organize itself in an enduring way purely spontaneously. It requires thought and planning ahead" (p. 56).

That first fall, together Ellen and I set up the blocks and areas for other materials. She was concerned about what rules she would need to establish. She was worried about letting children choose, so she devised a system of colored cards representing the different activities and she limited the number of children who could work at each area. But when children wanted a specific activity and the cards were all given out, they complained and felt left out. "But isn't that fair?" Ellen asked. "Look, if you can't build with blocks today, well, then you can do it tomorrow or the next day."

Inevitably with this system, children were excluded. I suggested that Ellen read *You Can't Say You Can't Play* (1992) by Vivian Paley. Paley tells how she involved her kindergarten in an exploration of the issues of exclusion that culminated in the new rule "You can't say you can't play." Enacting that rule had a profound and positive impact on the life of the children and their teacher.

It became clear to Ellen that democracy means that everyone has an equal opportunity. Everyone may not want a turn to paint, but everyone deserves the opportunity to do so even if the physical space limits the number who can paint at one time. Over time we discussed these ideas in many different ways, and Ellen began to ask the children, "Who wants to paint? Who wants to build?" in order to provide more opportunity for choice. The limits were set not by the teacher but by the situation.

One morning, for example, there was a lot of activity in the block area and buildings were being knocked down. Falling back on her old ways, Ellen declared, "Only four people can play in the blocks." We stepped aside and discussed these questions: Who owns the block area? How are problems solved in a community? Ellen decided to take the problem to the children, and she called a meeting. She said she had spoken too quickly when she made the decision for them. There was talk about the need to be more careful of others' buildings. Then one child said, "We need more space. It's too crowded." Ellen agreed. Looking at the area, she removed one of the two tables in an adjoining area and pushed the block shelf into that newly available space. "Now," she said, "we have a lot more space." Some children responded, "And we can all build now."

In a democratic community children care for and respect the materials themselves, just as the teacher cares for and respects the children. They build with blocks and put them away on labeled shelves without knocking them down; they take, and put away, clay from a container in which it is kept moist and handy; they paint with brushes and cups that they clean after use. The children share responsibility with the teacher for the maintenance of these materials—they have joint ownership of materials, activities, and how they live together. It is their classroom.

Do not imagine that this is a community without conflict. "I still confront the same behavior problems," Ellen told me in the spring, "but it doesn't affect me in the same way. I don't need to tell them what to do; now I talk to them. When you and I talk," she said to me, "you listen to everything I say. I said to myself, 'I have to listen to the children.'"

When children are having a hard time, she gives them a way out. She offers them another activity. On occasion a child has opted to lie down on a mat and has fallen asleep. Many children in this classroom live in impoverished environments where they are often exposed to stress and violence. They live very stressful lives.

What Is the Shared Work and Common Purpose of Teachers and Children?

Shared work and common purpose are the basic elements that form the cornerstone of community. Ellen has been able to build shared work and common purpose through a focus on social studies. She is listening to the children. They tell her that they are interested in their family life. They ask questions about growing up, play having a baby and going to a funeral, and build houses and churches.

One day at meeting, Ellen asked the children, "Who is in a family?" and "What does a family need?" She wrote their answers on chart paper. Because one of the things children mentioned that a family needs is food, she decided to initiate a study of the supermarket. What foods does it sell? How is the store organized? What jobs do people do in the store? To answer these questions, the class took a trip to a nearby supermarket. They interviewed the manager and the cashier. They wrote stories. They built a store in the block area and played supermarket. They had many meetings to explore and share children's ideas.

In her second year of teaching in New Beginnings, Ellen saw some children building with blocks and heard one child say, "We're building a neighborhood." And so a new social studies project began. "What is a neighborhood?" Ellen asked at their meeting. "What do you want to know about it?"

The neighborhood study led them, among other places, to the post office. The children wrote letters to one another. They saw the mail truck pick up the mailbags, which led them in turn to a study of trucks, cars, and other vehicles. One day the meeting was about traffic and "rules of the road." The group had just started talking about red and green lights when Clyde, who lives in a foster family, blurted out, "I don't have a dad." In the past, Ellen might have ignored his remark or said, "We're not talking about dads now." Instead, leaning forward with a serious expression, she offered concerned, silent support. She wanted the children to continue their ownership of the discussion. Two girls asked him, "Did he die?" Clyde shook his head. "Was he shot?" He shook his head. There was a giggle. Tyrone, indignant, said, "That's sad, not funny. Do you feel sad, Clyde?" He indicated yes. Tyrone continued, "Who watches you when your mama goes to church?" "I go with her." "Oh," Tyrone went on, trying to find a loving connection for Clyde, "Do you have a grandfather?" A no headshake. "How about another grandfather?" Another no. "A godmother?" Still no. "A cousin?" "Yes." There was an audible sigh of relief. Then a deep silence. Ellen was at a loss. This was heavy stuff. She looked at me for help. I said, "It looks like people are finished talking about this." Then Ellen guided them back to the topic of traffic. Now Clyde participated and offered that he knew something about parking in the right place or else you get a ticket. From here the children explored the meaning of "ticket." One child explained the difference between a ticket for the movies and a parking ticket.

For social studies to be meaningful, the teacher must know something about the lives of the children. What comprises their neighborhood? Do their parents have employment? What occupations do the children frequently see being performed? What concerns do they have? What do they care about? The children whose kindergarten I have been describing care about their families, about how babies are born, about what happens when someone dies, about how to care for animals, and about how plants grow. As Ellen helps them create a more and more caring community, they become increasingly able to bring their outside experiences into school. This provides for rich shared communication.

It takes time and thought to create a caring community of young children. One day, in our early work together, two children were building with blocks and got into a terrific row. Ellen and I moved in to help at the same time. Ellen asked me what to do. I asked her first to find out what the problem was and then to ask the two children for the solution. Each child described the conflict and then, in response to her question, decided to build separately rather than together. Through the shared work (building) and the shared purpose (to continue building), all three, teacher and two children, began to build a community.

This small event was a dramatic moment for Ellen. She understood how important it was to listen rather than to tell. During our first fall together, Ellen often lost patience with me because I seldom told her exactly what to do. By winter, however, she began to discover that children have the means to solve interpersonal problems when they receive a teacher's support and respect. According to Cuffaro (1995), Dewey asks the teacher to suspend the need for certainty, to accept the responsibility of freedom and choice, and to view self as capable of creating. This requires courage, initiative, a defined sense of purpose, intelligence, commitment, and perspective, particularly "the perspective that is born in hope and laughter" (p. 100).

As the choice of activities and the uses of open-ended materials became more familiar, the interactions among the children and between the children and Ellen began to change. Often, in the beginning, Ellen felt overwhelmed, not knowing what to do. As she listened to the children's play, as she helped them make decisions, as she provided them with more and more freedom, as she built a curriculum on their shared ideas, she gained in self-confidence.

There was a telling moment one afternoon that sums up Ellen's growing understanding of a democratic classroom. She had a teddy bear named Sadie. One child could take Sadie home each afternoon and bring her back the next day. This honor was bestowed on the boy or girl named "Super Kid of the Day," meaning that that child hadn't been involved in any conflicts during the day. I asked Ellen what would happen if a child never got to be "Super Kid of the Day"? "Oh, OK, Nancy, OK. I get it. Starting now, we'll do it alphabetically." A year later, a notebook went home with Sadie, too, so that parents could write any message they wanted in Sadie's book. Several parents drew their family tree. Some wrote short stories about their family. In this way parents began to come into the caring community.

THE GIFT OF TIME

The experience of working with Ellen as she began to develop a democratic community has been a high point of my long career in early childhood education. It was intensely gratifying to see that the principles I hold dear, respect for children's thinking, social studies as the core of the early childhood curriculum, and the use of materials for illuminating children's expressions, could be communicated so deeply to another person—all this, in a school that hadn't focused on professional development for teachers. I myself had only a surface relationship with the school administration that mostly just tolerated and accepted my presence. Never before had I seen a teacher so fully grasp the intentions of my supervisory work and willingly make such profound professional changes. It was a revelation to me that such a great turnaround could even occur.

The gift of time—we worked together for nearly 3 school years—was especially significant. Time gave us the opportunity to know one another well, to listen well to one another, and to build a trusting relationship—in short, to communicate. My style is not to tell a teacher what to do but rather to raise questions. Although that was sometimes frustrating for Ellen, it threw her back on her own resources. She discovered her own ability to think, which in turn boosted her self-confidence.

Over our 3 years together, Ellen saw how far she had come and she was very pleased with how she and the children were living in their kindergarten. Through our relationship—my respect for her ideas and my support and availability—she is becoming the kind of teacher she wants to be. Through our collaboration she has learned to create a caring, democratic community for and with children. The model of shared communication that I provided works for her, and she is finding that the same model works for and with the children.

9

An Oasis of Humanity
in a Sea of Bureaucratic Chaos

JOAN BOJSZA

Joan Bojsza is a Newark teacher for whom New Beginnings was not new. Instead, as she describes it, the project offered her a life pre-server, a way back to the thinking and doing that had been part of her original training as an early childhood educator. Bojsza's auto-biographical essay offers a moving portrait of an idealistic and dedicated professional who creates stimulating and supportive environments for young children year in and year out.

I WANTED TO BE a teacher since fourth grade. For girls born in 1949 and raised in strong, traditional families like mine, teaching or nurs- ing offered the only possibilities. Following the assassination of John F. Kennedy, filled with a commitment to social justice, I became pas- sionate about "saving the children." I secretly thought of becoming a teaching nun to be as fully self-actualized as President Kennedy had been in his sacrifice to our nation.

In high school I was president of the Future Teachers of America. We were an active chapter—going to college talks, visiting schools, and working with a local children's shelter. After graduation in 1967, I chose early childhood as a college major. The entire field was buzzing with talk about "age-appropriate" practices and bustling with Head Start and other initiatives spurred on by the Great Society. Teaching the whole child in a "unit approach" was the byword. "Play is the work of children" was the constant refrain. As one professor aptly quipped, "Some of these administrators need to learn that the ditto machine DID NOT come down on a thunderbolt."

Part of my student teaching was with a Head Start program in a poor rural region outside Washington, D.C., that had recently been desegregated. Some of the children lived in shacks that stood on stilts and did not have running water. Others lived in the same units in which their enslaved great-grandparents had lived. In many ways the families were still enslaved to poverty and lack of opportunity. The experience was an eye-opener and a motivator. A good teacher could change the life of a child.

I taught for 15 years before coming to Newark. Much of that time I spent on the "mommy track," working part time in a cooperative preschool that had strong affiliations with NAEYC and helped build my confidence as an early childhood professional. I was affirmed in my practice but eventually had to face fiscal reality. Our two daughters, 13 and 11, were fast approaching college age. I needed to teach full time.

In the spring of 1991, I sent out over 40 resumes but got only one offer. It was a blessing for me that the Newark schools were expanding to all-day kindergartens. I was told, "You have a job, but we don't know where yet." I was used to being an environment setter, going into school long before the official start in order to ready the room. Now I was held up in an office waiting to be assigned. Finally, on the third day of the fall semester, I was told to report to a school in the Central Ward. I went with a bag of tricks, but was dismayed to find that my classroom was in the basement at the end of a dark corridor. The facility was in desperate need of repair. I knew it was considered a brand new kindergarten, but I was flabbergasted to learn that meant a room with nothing for children. I asked about colored paper and blocks and was told, half in jest, "This is not the suburbs."

Luckily, my daughters were at an age when I could safely raid their old toys. Each day I loaded the car with puzzles, storybooks, table blocks, dress-up clothes, dolls, art supplies, puppets, Legos, boxes painted like sinks and stoves. I immediately got the reputation as the bag lady. Although they teased at first, the staff became supportive of my efforts, and the administration ultimately secured a grant to provide more materials. Even then I had to provide all the supplies for painting, snack, cooking, displays, curtains for broken closet doors, etc. I was given three reading workbooks, two math workbooks, and paced units to follow in content areas. These demands in academic skill work ran counter to what I was told when I was hired. What was going on? How was I to balance all this with what I knew about good early childhood practices?

That first year, well over a decade ago, was not easy. I digested the main ideas from the district manuals, tried to teach in small groups or centers, and spent over $1900 of my own money! Although the district, under the threat of state takeover and cited for inappropriate practices in the kindergartens, provided more materials in the succeeding years, it was still difficult to deliver a learner-centered program.

In late May 1996, I received a call from "downtown." The administration asked me to be part of a program, Project New Beginnings with Bank Street College, to become a model kindergarten teacher. Told I would receive state-of-the-art materials and be trained in the summer, I was awestruck. It was near the end of my fifth year in Newark, and the disparate demands of the system were pulling me apart. I felt that any change had to be for the better.

My first year in New Beginnings was extremely difficult. I increasingly felt like a square peg in a round hole. I had big plans and big anxieties. I wanted to get started quickly. Unfortunately, I found painters and carpenters in my classroom until the moment when the children arrived. I came in on a Sunday to try to make the room inviting for Monday morning. One worker remained to stain the closets. It was 95 degrees and the odor was enough to put you out. The room was a warehouse of boxes. I didn't have an inventory of the supplies, and opening each box set my head spinning with a new plan. But fortunately now I was swimming in materials—books, paper, blocks, manipulatives, furniture, etc. More items arrived sporadically throughout the year, and I had to magically fit them into my 125-year-old room with one small cabinet.

In my isolated position as one of the first 16 New Beginnings teachers, I had to try to satisfy district demands that were often in opposition to the thematic, integrated approach of the project. Weekly pacing reports, yearlong planning overviews, for which we were held accountable at the exact intervals indicated, and voluminous files of student work were mandated by the district. In addition, we never knew when the Yellow Bus—that is, the inspection team from downtown—would arrive to look at our student files, records, plans, overviews, and management strategies. All the paperwork felt repetitive and punitive. It seemed as if the state takeover was only robbing us of more teaching energy.

I persevered, with the guidance and example of a New Beginnings mentor who worked in my classroom every week. By the close of the year I felt affirmed. To be sure, there were growing pains and tears. I was challenged to give up contrived or cute hands-on activities and replace them with real choices that would not just ensure the basics but enable children to stretch and grow. I was also learning how to balance the things I could not change with my understanding, first developed as an undergraduate, that children learn best in meaningful frameworks and caring communities—the tenets of good early childhood education stood firm in the test of time. The project gave new validity and depth to my attempts to create age-appropriate curriculum.

The real turning point—that is, the point at which I knew that I was blessed to be part of this child-centered program—came in my second year with New Beginnings. I was at a workshop when Lesley Koplow, a social worker affiliated with the project, spoke about the development of children. She outlined how social and emotional trauma and unmet needs can arrest the cognitive development of children. At the close, she asked for questions. It was just about time to go and I was shy to speak, yet I had a burning statement to make. My heart was pounding as my hand went up. When called on, I don't know where the words came from but I spoke passionately, saying something like, "I see the faces of so many of my students in the scenarios you outlined. We write up problems and the needs of our students and all we are left with is volumes of paper. There is a snowball's chance in hell that any help or counseling will follow. What we need is a program to offer counseling and family therapy to our children. Until the social and emotional lives of the students are addressed, no longer ignored in the shadow of the almighty 'cognitive test,' we cannot really help them to learn. Perhaps Bank Street can create a program to assist us."

To my surprise, the response was overwhelming. I know I was red in the face and people asked me if I was crying. I remember someone coming up to me and saying, "Are you OK? You're absolutely right. You said what we were all thinking."

The real humanity of the project rests in the fact that our New Beginnings mentors began to push for the social and emotional interventions needed. They have facilitated working relationships with several area hospitals. In 1998, mental health consultants joined the New Beginnings staff. The children of Newark have many needs that had been brushed aside because of lack of funds or just plain denial. Finally, the project is helping us address them.

This year, my fourth as a New Beginnings teacher, I made a difficult choice. I decided to leave a school in which I had taught for 8 years to join a school with a stronger commitment to the project. Fortunately my assistant, Valerie Moss, consented to go with me. It was difficult to leave colleagues and families I had come to know so well. My New Beginnings mentor had long urged me to consider a move to this school where a nurse practitioner, a social worker, and professionals from a nearby hospital are more readily available. The physical task itself was a nightmare. I rented, loaded, and drove a U-Haul truck with my personal and Bank Street materials to the new location.

I believe now as I did in my college days that all children have a right to the best education possible—one that is age appropriate and addresses the whole child. The issue is one of social justice. The children of Newark deserve a quality, research-based education as much as other children do. My work with the project has affirmed my early educational commitment. The New Beginnings mentors have treated me as a "whole person." They have responded to my own social and emotional needs as well as supported my efforts to use new teaching strategies. Their friendship and the community of the project have enabled me to work with many children who live in extremely stressful circumstances. I am glad that I took the risk of moving to a school that is slated to become an all–New Beginnings school. The prospect of working with others of similar mind and dedication was the oasis of humanity I needed to move forward. For if one loses her ideals and integrity, what is left?

10

Working Together

LENORE FURMAN AND KATHLEEN HAYES

Lenore Furman is an experienced kindergarten teacher and one of the original 16 New Beginnings participants. Kathleen Hayes, formerly a classroom teacher at the Bank Street School for Children, is a New Beginnings staff developer. Together, this teacher–staff developer pair describe the changes in Furman's classroom over a 2-year period. The essay includes examples of relatively simple changes such as the introduction of a News of the Day Book *to build literacy and language skills and a family-style snack to support community in the classroom. It also describes the development of a sophisticated art curriculum that led to a series of four trips to the Newark Museum and the creation of a classroom museum to display the children's own work. The authors show how a small triumph, an administrator's permission to use public transportation, led to important learning for the children and other adults in the school.*

W ORKING TOGETHER is the hallmark of Project New Beginnings. Staff developers and teachers work together to change a teacher's practice. In addition, staff developers, teachers, and administrators must work together if child-centered classrooms are to be supported and sustained. It's a daunting task. In this chapter, we talk together about how and why it worked for us.

KATHLEEN: Before we began working together at Abington Avenue Elementary School, Lenore took a New Perspectives course on emergent literacy that I was teaching at Bank Street College. So, when

I arrived at Abington in 1997, I was surprised and pleased to see that she had implemented many of the suggestions from my course. It created an instant bond of trust. Here was someone who welcomes my help! That was incredibly reassuring as I struggled to make sense of my new environment.

LENORE: I first saw Kathleen at work when I observed in her 4–5's classroom at the Bank Street School for Children, long before we knew each other or had even the slightest notion that we would one day work together. Her gentle yet skillful way with children was impressive. She seemed to have a real sense of the children's abilities and needs. I watched as she sewed a binding on a book while having conversations with various children about the tasks in which they were engaged. With her thoughtful questions and responses, she helped them think about their work and extend their ideas.

September 2000 begins my 19th year of teaching. Sixteen of them have been at Abington. I taught first grade for a year and then taught half-day kindergarten for 9 years. In September 1995, a year before Project New Beginnings came to Abington, I switched to a full-day kindergarten program. At that time, my classroom had centers because I knew that children needed places where they could work on their own. However, I was required to make the district math and reading programs the central focus of my curriculum. As a result, my teaching was primarily whole-group instruction.

KATHLEEN: Having taught in a very child-centered school for many years, I found it hard to enter classrooms in Newark that were so teacher directed. I wanted teachers to change, and I wanted it to happen quickly. It was painful to watch and wait. Lenore was making changes more quickly than most. I couldn't understand why they were not willing to change, as she was. But gradually, I came to see that Lenore and I had shared common experiences, the course I taught and her visit to my classroom before I was a staff developer in the project. Before I even arrived, we had the basis for a relationship built on mutual respect and trust. The other teachers had not met me before I walked into their rooms. They had no idea whether I would be able to really help them. It was going to take time to develop that trust. In addition, they were hearing about New Beginnings for the first time. They needed at least a full year to internalize what they were being asked to do.

The longer I've worked in the project, the more reciprocal my work with teachers has become. They have taught me a great deal about how to teach students in an urban public school setting. They helped me discover the culture of the Newark Public Schools. As it had the teachers, it took me a year before I could really even begin to understand what they were telling me. They would say, "But Kathleen, that's the way it is here," and I would think, "I don't get it." I needed experiences of my own in Newark before I had an adequate context to understand what they were telling me. Gradually I began to "get it" just as they began to "get" what I was saying. By the end of a year, the teachers and I usually discover that we have enough of a common language and enough trust in one another to begin working fruitfully together.

LENORE: Abington is a Pre–K–8 school that serves about 1,000 students. The population is primarily working class. Many parents are eager to enroll their children at Abington because it has a solid reputation in the district. As a result, there are often between 24 and 30 children in a class. In 1998, when more teachers became part of Project New Beginnings, the administration provided aides in the K, 1, and 2 classrooms. They understood that there was a need to support and meet the needs of early childhood teachers.

KATHLEEN: I have met and worked with many teachers at Abington and throughout the district, who have tried to move from teacher-centered to child-centered classrooms. This has required a great deal of risk and hard work. I feel extremely privileged to have been able to support and witness the work that these teachers have done. The process that Lenore and I describe is illustrative of the work between many teachers and many staff developers.

LENORE: Once New Beginnings came to Abington, I began developing a more child-centered classroom. The very first change I made was to get rid of my teacher-made calendar in the meeting area. I wanted the children to have ownership of the activity. Each day a different child wrote the numeral on the calendar. I was beginning to let go.

KATHLEEN: Because Lenore had done so much work on the structure of her classroom, our work together could focus on ways to build community. I shared how, as a teacher, I began my day with an "arrival time" that gave children opportunities to talk together as they worked with a limited number of materials. I also explained how children could bring the "stuff" of their lives into the classroom by telling me their "news," which I wrote in a daily *News of the Day Book* and which I then read at morning meeting.

LENORE: After talking together, I realized that the morning arrival time was a significant transition between home and school. Before I began working with New Beginnings, I hadn't thought about ways to foster and support the children's conversation with one another. Kathleen's suggestion that I try using a *News of the Day Book* was very helpful. It's a powerful way to support children's talk together about things that matter to them.

As we talked about ways to support children's talk, Kathleen also helped me see that snack was another point in the day where I could encourage conversation between the children. I created a "family style" snack time, one where children set the tables and then passed the food to one another, so they learned how to ask one another for what they needed, for instance, "Pass the juice please." They also had to figure out how to share the food evenly. And our extended, sitting-down-together snack time gave children the opportunity to engage in meaningful conversation.

KATHLEEN: Lenore was interested in finding ways to build community in her classroom and she asked for help. But not all teachers are so clear. Some aren't sure what to ask of me. One of the ways I have found to make my work less threatening for them is to ask them to consider changing the way they develop nonacademic activities. Creating meaningful art experiences for children has been one of my most effective entry points into classrooms. With Lenore I talked about how to create a sequential art curriculum that allowed children to express their own ideas and feelings.

LENORE: Rather than just letting me do arts and crafts projects, often with a holiday theme, Kathleen helped me see that art materials were an important part of the ongoing curriculum and that my job as a teacher was to help children become skilled at using art materials. For example, when I introduced collage, I began with plain colored-paper collages. When they were skilled at cutting, tearing, and arranging paper shapes, I gave them patterned and plain paper, and then moved to rough and smooth fabric. This allowed children to become increasingly sophisticated in their work. After they had made many designs, I suggested they try making a collage that looked like something.

KATHLEEN: The design of the project supported and encouraged me to spend a great deal of time in teachers' classrooms. As a result, I was able to tailor my suggestions to what was actually happening in each room. As I watched the children begin to move toward representational collages, I showed Lenore how she could help children create people and animals from simple, cardboard geometric shapes. The children could then use collage materials to create clothing, facial features, fur, etc.

LENORE: As some of the children were making cardboard people and animals at the art center, other children were working in blocks and wanted people for their buildings. Kathleen suggested that I encourage the children to make their own people and animals for the block area. I discovered that the skills the children were learning in art could be put to good use as they busily set about making many small cardboard people and animals for our block area.

KATHLEEN: One of the things that so impressed me about those block people and animals was that Lenore asked the children to make them for the block center, rather than make their "own" accessories. Working together to create props for the block area was a powerful way to build community. She was thinking a lot about how to help the children become a supportive, caring community.

As we entered our third year of work together, Lenore wanted help to create more substantial integrated units of study. We had created an art curriculum that allowed children to freely explore paint, clay, and collage materials. I wanted them to discover that some adults work with those materials and that their artworks can be displayed in museums. For a couple of years, Lenore and I had talked about doing a series of trips to the Newark Museum. We decided the time had come!

As a teacher of 4- and 5-year-olds, I knew that taking multiple trips to the same site was beneficial for young children. They became confident "trip takers." They knew where they were going and what was expected of them. I was eager to take the children on four visits to the museum.

LENORE: As part of the children's pretrip activities, we asked them, "What do you know about museums?" and "What do you want to find out?" These discussions helped the children think about the questions that they wanted to ask the museum staff. We explained to them that we would visit the museum each Wednesday for the next 4 weeks. We helped them think and talk about what they might see.

I had prepared the children for the visits to the museum. Now I had to prepare the parents and the administration. I wanted to use public transportation. And I wasn't sure the school would let me take a large group of young children on the Newark subway.

KATHLEEN: One of my goals at Abington was to show the school administration the value of using public transportation, that it was safe to take children on trips using public transportation. The school is near a number of city bus routes and only a few blocks from the Newark subway. I knew that if teachers used it, they would be able to take children out much more frequently than if they had to rely on expensive school buses. The year before, the administration allowed a first-grade teacher, Sandra Snead, to use the city subway to visit Newark's Penn Station during her transportation study. It is important to use the environment for learning purposes. With that precedent, Lenore and I proposed taking her kindergarten class on four trips (one a week) to the Newark Museum, using the city subway. They agreed!

LENORE: I was excited about using public transportation for our trips, but I knew the administration would require many chaperones. I wasn't sure we would have enough volunteers because many of the parents worked. I sent a letter home explaining the museum study and the four trip dates, giving the parents the opportunity to volunteer for the date that was most convenient. The response was overwhelming. Some parents rearranged work schedules or secured babysitters so they could attend at least one trip. Several parents signed on for all four trips. This proved especially helpful because, as they became familiar with the trip routines, they were able to help first-time chaperones.

KATHLEEN: As the parents began to gather in the classroom before the first trip, I explained that we would visit three galleries and gave each parent a clipboard on which to record the children's comments as they viewed the art. Each parent would be responsible for his or her own child and two or three additional children. I stressed that we wanted them to interact with the children, to talk together about what they were seeing, both on the trip to and from the museum and while we were there.

When we arrived at the museum, we went immediately to the cafeteria and the children ate their bag lunches. (The museum doesn't open to the public until 12:30, so we had to plan the trip for the afternoon.) After lunch, we moved to the African gallery, where the curator and the security guard responded to the questions the children had prepared. We then moved with the children up to the second floor. We had decided to use three galleries filled with abstract American art for this first visit.

We talked with the children about the abstract paintings and asked them to describe the lines, colors, and shapes they saw, as we did back in the classroom when we talked with them about their own paintings. It was exciting to hear the children's comments. One child exclaimed, "Look how beautiful the colors are on the black. I want to try a painting like that!"

In one of the galleries there was a very large four-panel abstract mural. We lined children up in front of it to see how big it was—15 children standing in a row!—and talked about how the artist had filled the entire space with colored lines and shapes.

The museum staff gave us sketch boards, paper, and colored pencils. For the last 15 minutes of the visit, the children were invited to draw anything they wanted. Some children tried to copy what they saw. Nicholas was able to draw the colored lines he saw on a painting that somewhat resembled what the artist had done. Other children just filled their paper with a design of their own. We then packed up our supplies, retrieved the children's coats, and the children, staff, and parents headed back toward the subway. I stayed behind to go through the museum again, to determine what the children would see on their visit next week.

I found three galleries that would give them an opportunity to see very different materials. One gallery had boxes covered with a variety of materials; another was filled with small, beautifully crafted constructions of seashells, small rocks, and coral. The third gallery contained folk art, primarily stone sculptures by William Edmondson.

LENORE: For the second trip I decided to change the format. Instead of eating our lunch in the museum cafeteria, we had a picnic in our classroom before we left. This lightened our load on the subway because we didn't have to carry all those lunches. It also shortened the length of the trip.

I wanted the parents to have a guide to help them talk about the three exhibits we would visit, so I made a trip sheet. It included some art vocabulary and questions they might ask the children as they moved through the galleries. The trip sheet showed the parents how to focus the children's observations, and gave the children and the parents a common language to use as they discussed the art together.

The children were interested in all three galleries, but they were particularly drawn to the seashell exhibit. One child, looking at a construction, exclaimed, "Look at the angel!" Another child, observing the same construction, said, "Oh, what a beautiful butterfly." The boxes, decorated with an assortment of household objects, were intriguing to the children. Some said they wanted to decorate boxes too. The stone sculptures were less ambiguous than the seashell constructions. The children were quick to describe what they saw as they looked at them.

KATHLEEN: Unfortunately, I was unable to accompany the group that day. But after hearing how successful the second trip was, the question was where to go next. Finally, we decided to bring the children to the 20th-century American landscapes and portraits. We would walk past the galleries we visited on our first trip to get to them. I thought it would be a helpful reminder of our first trip, and I thought the paintings would engage the children. We prepared a trip sheet for the parents. We also shared with them *Come Look With Me: Exploring Landscape Art with Children* (1992) by Gladys S. Blizzard. It gave the parents some insights into the types of paintings that the children would see.

As I was walking with a group of three children through the galleries, we came upon some representational paintings by Georgia O'Keefe. On the first trip, a Georgia O'Keefe painting of a white flower had captivated one of the girls in my group. She had proudly drawn a "copy" of the painting when we gave her drawing materials. As we walked into a gallery on this trip, she cried out, "Look, it's like the flower one!" She had spotted another painting by O'Keefe. She was thrilled to find a painting that produced the same emotional intensity for her. I was glad we had returned to painting. Clearly, the repeated visits were having the desired effect. The children were becoming skilled observers of art.

I realized that part of the value of this series of trips was that we had introduced the museum to many parents. Some of them had heard that the museum contained a mini-zoo, and they were eager to see it. We decided that our final trip would be to see the zoo. Although we had thought the entire series of visits would focus on art, it was clear that we had to be responsive to the interests and enthusiasm of the parents.

We decided to make our last trip an easy, celebratory trip. I encouraged Lenore to bring a large play parachute so we could play in the park after our brief visit to the mini-zoo. It was a wonderful way to end our visits. The children were excited to see the animals, they walked past some of the art they had seen on previous visits, and they left, confident that they knew a great deal about their city museum.

LENORE: Our weekly Wednesday afternoon trips to the museum had met our goals. The children had learned a great deal about the museum, they became thoughtful observers of art, and they became confident trip takers. What we didn't expect was that our journeys out into the city streets would expose the children to so much more.

As we walked from the subway stop to the museum, we passed a church undergoing renovation. On our first trip, we saw a worker sanding the front door. The next week, we were surprised to discover that he was still there. This time he was applying stain. Each week we watched the progress of the renovation.

After our first visit, as we headed back to the subway, we saw a postal worker emptying a mail storage box into his mailbag. The next week, we saw him again! We said, "We saw you here last week!" and he said that he remembered us. The children asked him what he was doing and he told them.

The regularity of our trips gave us the opportunity to discover the patterns of life and work on the streets. Sometimes we saw the same people at work. Sometimes we just remembered who had been working the previous week but wasn't there now, such as the window washer. The children were beginning to make sense of the life of the community on the walk to and from the museum. It was an unexpected bonus for all of us.

Back in the classroom, the children were eager to try out some of the ideas they had gathered from their visits to the museum. We decided to make their decorated boxes, so I sent home a letter requesting cigar boxes and various small items that could be glued onto the boxes and would be shared by the group. The cigar boxes were hard to find. One parent did some legwork and brought in about 12 for us. The small items that the children gathered were imaginative and interesting. It was clear that both the children and their parents had thought carefully about what to bring. The objects included small stones, colored popsicle sticks, plastic letters, beads, checkers, buttons, and small toys.

First the children covered their boxes with collage materials. We had done a lot of collage work during the year, so the children were familiar with this technique and they used the materials with confidence. Then they made choices about which items would be used on their boxes. It was interesting to observe as the children found many ways to make lid handles using different materials.

As the children made new clay sculptures, black-pencil drawings, colored-pencil drawings, constructions, and paintings, we used an expanding art vocabulary to discuss their work. We talked about line, color, and shape as well as about whether pieces were abstract or representational. We read trade books to help focus our discussions of these concepts (Blizzard, 1990; Micklethwait, 1993; Yenawine, 1991abcd). The children became familiar with the terminology and often used these words to describe their work.

KATHLEEN: As Lenore worked with the children on various types of constructions and clay sculptures, I was eager to see if the children could work together in small groups to make panels for their own large-scale mural. Throughout the year the children had painted, using primary colors to mix a rich palette for their individual paintings. I gave them very large sheets of butcher paper and, after some experimentation, determined that working on the floor was the best way for four children to paint on the large piece of paper. As they worked, they needed help to avoid painting over someone else's work. On subsequent days, smaller numbers of children worked on two additional panels. It was easier for two or three children to find spaces to do their "own thing" without painting over someone else's work, as happened on the first panel.

As I watched the children create rich works of art, clearly inspired by their visits to the museum, I was anxious to showcase their work. The end of the year was fast approaching, including the Kindergarten Celebration to which all the parents were invited. I hoped that Lenore would consider turning her classroom into a museum, so the children could hang or display their work and invite the parents to come to the "opening" on the day of the Kindergarten Celebration.

LENORE: When Kathleen suggested we turn the classroom into a museum, I had some reservations. I was excited about the idea, but I wondered if this was too big a task to attempt for the last day of school. It meant selecting children's work to be displayed, putting away materials, rearranging the classroom furniture to form galleries, mounting artwork on walls, shelves, and tables, and labeling all the pieces. It would be a very big job. But I decided to try it. I knew it would be a powerful culminating activity for both the museum study and the school year. Mrs. Lugo, my aide, and I put everything in motion and, in 2 days, transformed the classroom into a museum.

I sent the parents a letter inviting them to visit the classroom museum when they brought their children to school for the kindergarten program. There was great enthusiasm as the children proudly showed their work. Everyone moved thoughtfully around the room observing the art and taking pictures. It met all my expectations and was a wonderful way to end a year that had been centered on building a classroom community.

KATHLEEN: Like Lenore, I was thrilled at how successful the multiple visits to the museum and the creation of the classroom museum had been. I have a tendency to "push" teachers. Sometimes I push too hard and it backfires. This time, it worked. We had talked for many years about how to turn the "kindergarten graduation ceremonies" into ceremonies that celebrate children's actual classroom experiences and work. And now we had found a way to do just that.

LENORE: Working with Kathleen these past 3 years has been both a pleasure and a privilege. She has helped me look inside myself to examine the "whys" and become a much more reflective teacher. In her usual sensitive way, just as I observed her do with her 4–5's students, she has helped me extend my thinking, become a more astute observer of children, and more adept at meeting the needs of my students by carefully planning curriculum.

KATHLEEN: Working with Lenore these past 3 years has been both a pleasure and a privilege as well. I marvel at her willingness to ask hard questions of herself and of me. She has helped me grow in my understanding of teaching as I watch her work, gently, skillfully, and oh-so-patiently with young children, many of whom might be labeled "at risk" in other settings but who end up feeling empowered and at home in her classroom.

I have learned much about the art of teaching in Lenore's classroom. She has become a mentor teacher for me and for her colleagues in Newark. She brings hope to the children and their families, to discouraged colleagues and staff developers alike. She helps young children discover that they can work together in a caring community, learn what they need to learn, and, most important, learn what they want to learn.

11

Being Like Me: What Newark's School Children Say About Identity

LESLEY KOPLOW

In this essay, Lesley Koplow, coordinator of the mental health initiative for Project New Beginnings, documents her work in one second-grade classroom. Here the children learn to ask difficult questions about extra-classroom experiences, express the full range of emotions that these sometimes unsettling events evoke, and witness a teacher–staff developer team who are ready to listen and respond to their deepest concerns.

THEY KNOW ME. I am the lady who comes in to read to them about anything they might be worrying about. I have been coming for 2 years and they are comfortable with me—sitting, reading, talking, exploring, and helping them feel safe at school. I am familiar to these 7-year-olds, but I am aware of the ways that I am different. The most obvious is that when I am with them, I am the only White person in the room.

One morning, at the group's request, we read a story about a little boy who doesn't know his daddy. The boy in the story appears to be Latino. Much discussion and personal comment follows from the story.

Jason asks abruptly, "Aren't Black people special?" "What do you mean?" I inquire. "Well, only White people go to work every day and Black people just hang out." The teacher, Ms. Adams, is also African-American. "How about me?" she asks. "I'm working!" "But you don't work in one of those big office buildings downtown," Jason replies. Ms.

Adams assures Jason that, in fact, many African-American people work in the big office buildings downtown. She will take them on a field trip to see this. Then Ms. Adams asks the group, "What do you think about what Jason is saying? Are Black people special?"

Many children raise their hands to counter Jason's assertion. "There are a lot of important Black people," Rhonda says. "Like President Clinton." Ms. Adams looks surprised. "Is President Clinton Black?" she asks. The kids are divided. "Why do you think that President Clinton is Black?" Ms. Adams asks Rhonda. "Because he likes Black people," answers Rhonda. "Well, President Clinton is good to Black people, and his best friend Vernon Jordon is Black, but President Clinton is White," Ms. Adams clarifies.

Another boy, Michael, raises his hand. "I know why Black people don't have jobs. It's because White people give them drugs so they can act stupid so then the White people can have all the power." I wonder about Michael articulating this theory in my presence. He does not seem inhibited by the fact that I am White. This is a good example of how an African-American teacher and White staff developer work together to combat young children's stereotypes/misunderstandings about race. Such work can only occur if the children feel comfortable enough in the classroom to express their ideas, no matter how uncomfortable they make us, the adults, feel. Otherwise, how else to know where to begin!

When the discussion has come to an end and I am getting ready to leave, Tina follows me to the door to make her weekly request. "Read about being afraid of Muslims. I keep telling you to find a book about being afraid of Muslims."

"It's hard to find a book about being afraid of Muslims," I say. "Maybe next week we can write our own story about that." I think about Tina's persistent request. She has let me know that she was frightened by an incident with a Muslim woman whom she passed on the street. What would the other children have to say about this?

The next week I tack paper to the easel in preparation for our group story. "Most of you know Tina's story about the Muslim ladies in the car. Tina was passing by and got scared. Let's write the story down, and then we can think of different ways that the story can end. The kids enthusiastically supply the details of Tina's experience. "Once upon a time there was a girl named Tina. She walked by a car with some Muslim ladies inside. She saw a baby in the car. She waved to the baby but the mother got mad. The mother gave Tina a threatening look. Tina ran away."

I decided to add to the story myself. "Then Tina ran into a grocery store. She wanted to buy some potato chips, but the chips were on a high shelf and she couldn't reach them. A Muslim lady was shopping in the store. She saw Tina and came over and helped her by reaching the chips and handing them to her. Tina went home and went to bed. Before falling asleep, she was thinking about the different experiences she had with Muslim people that day. She thought . . ."

"That's where I'm going to end the story. Now you can each write something about how you think Tina felt about things."

"I'm not taking no chips from no Muslim lady!" Tina protests loudly. "Well, you can write that if you want to," I say.

"Tina!" Ms. Adams calls out. "You told me you want to be a psychiatrist when you grow up. How are you going to be a psychiatrist if you don't like people who are different from you? What will happen if a little Muslim girl comes to you for help?"

"Yeah, Tina," Aisha chimes in. "What if a kid comes to you because she's afraid of Muslims? What will you do then?"

Tina shrugs her shoulders. "I'll write a little story like this one, I guess!" Ms. Adams and I smile at each other. The kids ask some questions about why Muslim women wear black clothing and why their clothing covers their entire body. Ms. Adams answers their questions simply and informatively, leaving them to their writing.

When I return the next week, the children proudly read their stories to me. I listen, then collect them and make a book with their story outcomes for the classroom. Some of the stories are conciliatory. "Tina thought that some Muslim people are nice because the woman gave her the potato chips." Many of the stories expressed wariness and projected negative events into the plot, treating the appearance of a second Muslim woman as an indication that danger would follow. "Tina thought that she better hide before that Muslim woman came and tried to take her away." "Tina thought the Muslim lady in the store was the mean Muslim lady's daughter, and then when she got home her mother told her that Tina waved at the baby and they didn't like her anymore."

Ms. Adams often asks me about my daughter in the presence of her class. "Bring a picture of her to show us!" they demand. I always agree but for many weeks don't remember to include a photograph in my bag as I pack to leave in the morning. Finally, I remember to bring a picture of my 3-year-old daughter. I wonder how they will comment on her appearance, since her hair is much lighter than mine and her eyes are blue while mine are brown. The children flock around me, studying the image of my daughter playing at her grandparents' house. "You can ask me questions if you want to," I say.

"Is she African-American or Puerto Rican?" asks Erica immediately. I am speechless for a moment, surprised at the question. "She is

Caucasian," I say. "She was born in New Jersey." With this clarification, they go on to ask a number of other questions. "Does she have a babysitter?" "Does she go to school?" "How old is she?" "Does she have her own room?" "Is she afraid of the dark?" When I confirm that she sleeps in her own room and at times is scared of the dark, they make numerous suggestions about getting her night lights, and putting lights on in the hallway to help her feel better. Being afraid is a topic we have explored as a group many times over the last 2 years. Many of the children have had terrifying experiences that occurred at night and are frightened of darkness. At this point children realized that all children might be afraid of the dark.

When I think about what these second graders are telling me about how race and identity issues interact for them, I am compelled to write as a way of sharing their perceptions as well as clarifying the meaning of their messages for myself. Because I have become familiar to them and I am attentive to their emotional well-being, perhaps I am perceived to be "related"—part of the school family. My daughter's white skin and blue eyes are not the key to her racial identity. Instead, because I am taken in as being "related" to them, and my daughter is related to me, the children see her as being under their own umbrella—as being "someone like me" and, therefore, African-American or Puerto Rican. The kids see President Clinton as a friend to Black people. He is then seen as Black himself.

A few weeks later, a White teacher in the school shares an anecdote with me that sheds further light on what I am hearing. A 6-year-old girl in her class approached the teacher saying, "Excuse me. I don't want to start trouble or nothing, but he (pointing to another child) called you White." Annie, who has very fair skin replied, "But I am White!" "No you're not," the girl answered. "You're light skinned!"

How do early childhood professionals understand this story? Is it another example of the comfort of seeing the familiar other as "being like me," or does it imply that being White has negative connotations and, therefore, is not an appropriate way to refer to someone for whom they care? But then there is the story of Tina and the Muslim lady, someone Black like them, but who is unfamiliar to them personally and unfamiliar in her dress and custom. Although she was also African-American, she is seen as someone "not like me" and, therefore, potentially dangerous. Possibly being Muslim had negative connotations to various children in the classroom, but when the group talked about Muslims, it seemed that the children knew little about them and had not much to say about prior experiences or parental opinions. The discussion in the classroom seemed to precipitate exploration about identity issues within the group. Indeed, a week after our story about Tina and the Muslim ladies, Andrea greeted me when I walked into the room, saying, "You know what? I told my mama the story about Tina being afraid of Muslims and she said I was Muslim too! I never knew that before!"

When I think about the ways that these children formulate constructs concerning race and identity, I think about the representational drawings of children between the ages of 3 and 7. The younger the artist, the more he or she is likely to draw on the basis of internal images of experience: how things seem as opposed to how they are. Therefore, the child who draws his brother having a tantrum colors him red and makes him as large as the house that surrounds him. The young child who draws a picture of the most comforting room in his house colors the walls like a rainbow and draws himself eating an ice cream cone. Children over 7 become less likely to do this. The 8-year-old artist is more likely to depict the tantrumming child with whatever hair color the child actually has, and a size relative in proportion to the rest of the drawing. The older sister of the young artist who draws her favorite room says, "But our walls are painted white and we're only allowed to eat ice cream in the kitchen!" The actual demands of the situation eventually become more compelling and more defining than one's own subjective experience (Mitchell & David, 1992).

Perhaps the children in Ms. Adam's second-grade class are telling us something about their developmental process in exploring identity issues and coming to feel safe with others who are different from them. Their current working premise seems to be, "People who become familiar and connected to us are like us." Actual differences are "painted with a tiny brush" and become a small part of the metaphorical picture. "People who are different but are unfamiliar and disconnected from us are potentially dangerous." Differences are painted with a giant brush and the metaphorical picture includes negative projections.

What are the implications of these observations for early childhood professionals? How can people who hope to help children strengthen their own identities and also celebrate diversity use the voices of Ms. Adam's second-grade class to inform their practice? How will these children's perceptions change as they move to third, fourth, and fifth grade?

Looking at constructs of sameness and difference as they relate to identity issues through a developmental lens is an important precursor for understanding children. But the strongest message for me has been the need to let children voice their perceptions so that we know what they are. If teachers rush in too quickly in an effort to help their students to become inclusive, they risk superimposing a curriculum about differences on a developmental foundation that is not yet strong enough to support it. On many occasions I have been surprised by what the kids have had to say. Too often I have assumed them to be in a more sophisticated place than our spontaneous open-ended conversations reveal. Listening to Jason, Rhonda, Aisha, Tina, and Erica, I confirmed my commitment to allow the children to speak their minds before I speak mine.

PART III

WORKING TOGETHER

D URING YEARS 4 AND 5 of Project New Beginnings, three sets of concerns—institutionalization, burnout, and inquiry-based curriculum—loomed large in the thinking of staff and teachers. None of these issues is new, but all take on an added urgency with the passage of time and the uncertainties of foundation support.

In years 3 and 4, New Beginnings largely assimilated to the Newark Public Schools literacy agenda and the needs of teachers to fulfill it. With the transformation of work periods that once included open-ended materials into "literacy blocks," the substitution of required early-morning journal writing for quiet games and table-top toys, and the replacement of group meetings with skills-building exercises, New Beginnings staff consider how to refocus attention on the project's educational commitment. That is, how can the achievement of literacy skills be placed in a broader context of helping young children to make sense of their lived experiences? How can New Beginnings be more effective in helping teachers create and sustain emergent curriculum that reflects children's interests and questions about the world around them?

From the project's perspective, the answers to these and other questions in large part rely on moving beyond loosely organized "thematic" integrations of subject matter to a more conceptually based understanding of curriculum. Here the integration of the disciplines is not imposed from the outside through a teacher-selected theme such as "apples" or "fall" but emerges from a study that itself requires the use of math and science, reading and social studies (Cohen, 1972; Mitchell & David, 1992). Blachly and Heintz, Furman and Hayes, Wagman and Reaves, and Balaban in this volume offer good examples of teachers moving toward more authentic integrations of curriculum.

Prompted to seek new ways to foster integrated, inquiry-based curriculum as well as a concern for future sustainability, in years 4 and 5 the project explored alternative staff development strategies including short- and long-format courses, yearlong social studies and science workshops, and site-based study groups. The reliance on a single format of service delivery, one-on-one classroom support, was no longer adequate. A more comprehensive set of strategies responsive to the needs of new and experienced New Beginnings teachers and to schools committed to a range of comprehensive school reform models was required. Putnam and Borko (2000) confirm the limits of staff development in the classroom setting:

> The situative perspective helps us to see that much of what we do and think is intertwined with the particular contexts in which we act. The classroom is a powerful environment for shaping and constraining how practicing teachers think and act. Many of their patterns of thought and action have become automatic—resistant to reflection or change. Engaging in learning experiences away from this setting may be necessary to help teachers "break set"—to experience things in new ways. (p. 6)

In addition to the new formats, the project secured Newark Public Schools professional development credits for teachers who participated in New Beginnings activities and district substitutes for teachers who wanted to visit other schools. In the fifth year, the district permitted teachers to attend New Beginnings workshops on school-wide staff development days.

The school reform literature documents the difficulties of projects such as New Beginnings that undertake broad changes in classroom organization (McLaughlin, 1976). New Beginnings classrooms with multiple centers, with thematic and emergent curriculum, and with attention to individual learning styles require teachers to put in many additional hours planning and gathering resources. They also require teachers to be continually assessing and reflecting upon their work. To put it simply, not all teachers are willing or able to sustain this high level of engagement. Over time, life trajectories—a new baby, an acrimonious divorce, the need to earn additional income—lead professionals to make different investments in their work.

Securing district professional development credits for involvement in New Beginnings activities and restructuring service delivery methods were part of the concern for bolstering teacher commitment. Importantly, staff developers also encouraged teachers to participate in extra classroom activities such as school-wide reform committees and professional organizations as well as to present workshops during staff development days. Hoyle (1989) refers to educators who perceive their work more narrowly in terms of classroom activities alone, their expertise based on years of experience and intuition, as possessing a restricted professionality. "Restricted" is not a comment on competence but rather on scope of activities. In contrast, teachers who are identified with an extended professionality locate their work within the broad social contexts and in relation to school policies and goals. They value collaboration and involvement in nonteaching professional activities.

Extended professionality is inherent to the developmental-interaction approach, which defines the teacher as a decision maker whose work is ideally informed by a balance of theory and practice (Nager & Shapiro, 2000). It also identifies the teacher as someone who works collaboratively with other professionals and community members to construct socially relevant curriculum. Research indicates that settings offering greater opportunities for experienced teachers to take on leadership roles are often more conducive to curricular change (Silin & Schwartz, 2000). Here teacher–staff developer relationships are deepened through frequent meetings outside the classroom as they work together on projects to benefit the entire school.

The essays in Part III, Working Together, attend directly to the business of bridging the distances between individuals and cultures, to the deepening relationships between schools and change agents. Prominent in the thinking of many of these authors is the question of race. Felice Wagman, for example, a White middle-class "Jewish girl from the suburbs," and Mary Reaves, a middle-aged African-American paraprofessional, describe how they transformed their improbable pairing into an unusually close personal and professional relationship. In supporting her four coauthors as they give voice to their experiences as children, parents, and paraprofessionals, Margot Hammond shows why successful research and reform is always a two-way street, one on which all parties are changed by their interactions. Judy Lesch's mindful essay examines how her expectations as a White, middle-class staff developer caused miscommunication and misunderstanding with the working-class African-American teachers to whom she was assigned, and Augusta Kappner, president of Bank Street, offers her perspective on making public–private ventures work. The closing essay by Eileen Wasow, herself an African-American and a Bank Street faculty member, describes the unexpected difficulties she encountered adapting to the needs of Newark teachers. In her mediation on difference, Wasow explores her own upbringing under the tutelage of a grandmother's "fierce" love, progressive educational environments that encourage agency, choice, and self-determination, and new scientific research on the role of early nurture. As a group, the chapters in Part III examine the processes through which differences are acknowledged and accommodated, trust is established, and the work of individual and institutional change is brought about.

12

Putting a Little Bass in Your Voice

Felice Wagman and Mary Reaves

*Felice Wagman, formerly a Newark classroom teacher, is a mental
health consultant with Project New Beginnings. Mary Reaves is a
30-year veteran of the Newark Public Schools. Their dialogue
illumines how a recent convert to progressive education explains her
work to someone with a more traditional educational commitment.
It also attests to the potential for collaboration across race and class
differences that may be found in New Beginnings classrooms.*

Felice: Seven years ago, my car was stolen in Newark's South Ward
while I was attending an after-school staff development class. To
quote the police officer who took my report that night, "You're in
the belly of the beast. Don't stop at any red lights. Get out of the
city as fast as you can."

Six years later, I found myself arranging a transfer from Lincoln Elementary School to Clinton Avenue Elementary School,
which happened to be located in none other than the South Ward.
I wanted to teach in a school fully committed to Project New Beginnings. But in the summer before I began my first year at Clinton,
some anxiety began to set in. How was I to cope with this new
environment? After all, the neighborhood in which I had worked
for the last 10 years, the West Ward's Vailsburg section, is quite
different from the South Ward. Vailsburg is a quiet, working-class
area characterized by row houses and a large West Indian immigrant community. Many families mow their lawns and plant flow-

ers in their yards. Some teachers consider this to be a more desirable place to work because of the higher level of parent involvement and lower incidence of behavioral problems. The contrast with the South Ward is striking. With dilapidated housing and adults loitering near the school during the middle of the day, it is a visibly depressed area. Also, because Clinton Avenue is a main thoroughfare, there is much more traffic and noise directly in front of the school and safety is a major issue.

For someone like me, a 30-something girl from the suburbs, all of this was a little intimidating. Besides, I knew no one in the school and to top it all off, I was newly pregnant with my first child. Would I be able to rely on anyone for help? Would I just have to, as always, count on myself? Would I fit into the school culture?

As fate would have it, the answer to this question lay in the appointment of one Mary Reaves, a 50-ish African-American woman, as my classroom aide. Mrs. Reaves was instrumental in easing my professional and social transition into Clinton Avenue School. More important, she made my teaching and bonding experience with the children and their parents all the more meaningful.

Before Project New Beginnings entered my life in 1996, I was a traditional teacher. For 9 years I had taught K–3 at Lincoln Elementary School, standing at the board with my students quietly sitting in rows listening to me. After 2 years of New Beginnings staff development, my teaching practices had changed dramatically. My classroom was now arranged in centers where children could choose where they wanted to go. The curriculum was age-appropriate, and I developed it by listening to kids and finding out about their interests. By the end of my second year, I was sold on the New Beginnings approach. At my other school I was one of only two project teachers and now I wanted to work in an environment where the New Beginnings philosophy prevailed in the school.

In time I secured a transfer to Clinton Avenue School where I was offered a kindergarten position. I had mixed feelings about Clinton. Although it was a pilot school with many New Beginnings programs in which I was eager to participate, I was concerned about fitting in. This became evident even before school started when, one day in the late summer, I brought some of my materials to my new classroom. The principal asked a teacher to direct me to the parking lot and introduce me to some of my new colleagues. The teacher frowned and said that we had to do it quickly because she wanted to get back to her lunch. Her brusqueness put me off. In new situations, I tend to be shy and introverted. I wondered if I would be able to develop a good working relationship with her or any other faculty.

Ironically, I soon learned that some of my perceptions of myself contrasted sharply with those of my colleagues. In fact, when school began, a new colleague warned, "People think you're too demanding and a princess. Lie low for a while and do your job. If you don't participate in the gossip here, you'll be OK." I thought about her comments and realized that a plan of action was needed. If I was going to succeed at Clinton, then I would have to improve my social skills. Though I wanted my peers to like me and respect my work with the children, I also concluded that making my classroom a safe and wonderful place for my students to learn was paramount. "Lying low" for a while, I was determined to focus on my classroom and keep away from social situations.

I had a challenging task ahead, and it was Mrs. Reaves who helped me get through it. When we first met, she was delivering supplies to my room. After she introduced herself and we exchanged pleasantries, I bombarded her with my concerns. I wanted to know if someone would be able to help me set up the classroom. I needed to rearrange the furniture into work areas as well as organize and label the children's materials before school started. I was worried that I wouldn't have much time to get all this done. I also complained that the custodians hadn't removed an enormous pile of trash that was sitting in the block area. I told her that I couldn't set up the blocks properly and asked if she knew when the custodians would get around to cleaning it up. She told me not to worry and that she would try to get some help.

Mrs. Reaves had been working at Clinton Avenue for a long time and she was well regarded. People listened to her and respected her point of view. As I later learned, she told the custodian, "That's my room. You have to treat that girl right until I tell you that you don't have to." Within the hour, my floor was spotless. Mrs. Reaves had begun to look out for me!

MARY: I had worked at Clinton Avenue as a teacher's aide for more than 20 years before Felice joined the faculty. I know many staff members there, some of whom have been my friends for a long time. We see each other at church as well as weddings and funerals. The Newark area has been my home since 1968, but I was born and raised in South Carolina. I have been married for 31 years and I am blessed with two children, one stepdaughter, and five grandchildren.

I had heard many things about Felice before she came to Clinton. I had worked with her previous principal and vice-principal and considered them friends as well. They told me that I would love working with Felice. However, some people in the Newark system made other kinds of comments such as, "Well she's OK but she's a little pushy"; "She likes things her way"; or "I don't know if the two of you will get along."

When I met Felice, my first impression was that she wore really short skirts and had a "Ms. Thang" attitude going on. She struck me as being a little full of herself. I was also concerned that the students might not respect or obey her. Kids at Clinton are not apt to take young, Barbie-like teachers seriously. While they have seen Caucasians and are drawn to the different hair texture and color as well as skin coloring, I expected them to be more concerned with getting to know why she is the way she is. Despite my concerns, I was committed to working together with her. After all, we both wanted the best for our students.

FELICE: In September, Mrs. Reaves and I spent a lot of time getting to know one another and conversing about how we were going to begin the year. We often met during preps and after school. It was important to me to build a relationship with her and include her as I developed my idea about teaching. I was worried that she would think that I took too much time teaching routines and establishing classroom community and not enough time on the academics. But Mrs. Reaves understood early on why I approached teaching in this way. I remember saying, "I am going to teach table painting for the first couple of days. I am going to show you and the kids how to do it. I'll do it today, and if you feel comfortable . . ." Mrs. Reaves interrupted, "Well, I don't know if I will feel comfortable." So I sat down at the table for a couple of days and I taught table painting, and then she said, "OK, I am ready to teach and I am ready to start. I can do this. The kids and I are not going to get messy. They can set up their own trays . . . yeah, this is something I can do. This makes sense and it's easy for the kids to understand." That was a powerful moment for us. I think Mrs. Reaves felt confident in her teaching ability and respected me for not rushing the process. This is particularly important because when teaching routines, the details really count. It makes for a safe classroom environment.

Together, we began building a classroom community. There was never a hierarchy of power. We always made a conscious effort to make sure we were equal partners in the classroom. We intended to send a clear message—Mrs. Wagman and Mrs. Reaves are the teachers in this classroom. If Mrs. Reaves says no to a child, it is no. If Mrs. Wagman says no to a child, it is no. We always backed each other up.

MARY: At the beginning, Felice and I had different ways of handling discipline problems in the classroom. I often thought she was a softy, and I would tell her to put a little bass in her voice to discipline the kids. She informed me that she didn't like to yell, to which I replied, "Don't yell. . . . Get down and then it will come out and they know you mean business. The kids think you look too soft. They are enamored with your look. They don't respect you." Reluctantly, she added a little bass to her voice and, surprisingly, she did have more control of the kids. I told her, "If you say it that way and sound like their mother or grandmother, then they'll listen to you. That's what they're used to." Felice once told me that in her house, when she was growing up, if someone raised their voice, she *knew* she was in a heap of trouble. She thought if she handled discipline in this manner, the kids would be frightened of her.

FELICE: Mrs. Reaves and I had a lot of conversations about the kids' behavior. Some would scream at quiet time, hit, curse, and throw tantrums during the course of the day. When do you punish or do you punish at all? I told Mrs. Reaves that I thought that there were always reasons for the children's behavior. We had to think about why a particular child acted out.

Mrs. Reaves began to understand my point of view when an incident occurred with Tekiya. Tekiya was taking extra donuts and putting them in her book bag. Mrs. Reaves came over to me and asked what she should do. I explained to her that Tekiya was having a hard time at home. Her parents were preoccupied with other concerns and her grandmother had become the mainstay of the family, struggling to keep all the children fed. I told Mrs. Reaves to listen to me as I talked to Tekiya. "Tekiya," I said, "I see that you put the donuts in your book bag. You must be really hungry. If you're hungry and would like an extra snack, come and tell Mrs. Reaves or me. We will always have extra snacks for you." I could have screamed at Tekiya for taking the donuts and made her cry. I could have punished her by keeping her in from lunch. However, it was my job to let Tekiya know that we would meet her needs and that she'd be safe in our classroom. Tekiya often asked for an extra snack during the school year, and she never stole again. Mrs. Reaves and I never discussed this pivotal event until this summer on the phone.

MARY: We had one especially difficult moment together. When we talked about it this summer, I began the conversation saying, "Felice, I really learned a lot from you. Remember that Tekiya incident? I knew her family well. I had her brother. He was difficult. And I was ready to get tough with Tekiya and you handled it differently. You're special and I learned a lot from you. I love you."

FELICE: One of the highlights of our daily routine was the morning meeting. This time was always characterized by lively conversation. However, Mrs. Reaves and I disagreed about what topics should be discussed. I encouraged children to talk about what was on their minds, about the things that were important to them. Some experiences such as the birth of a sibling or move to a new apartment were easier to talk about than others—the death of a family member or drugs and violence in the community. One morning a child was going on and on about a monster. Privately, Mrs. Reaves asked me why I was letting him talk so much. I told her that I thought he needed to let it out and that other children in the group had similar fears. Everyone would benefit from sharing their worries. Mrs. Reaves told me that she wasn't brought up to discuss these kinds of issues.

MARY: I guess it goes back to the old school. My mom always says to continue talking about something makes it more vivid in the mind, and some things are just best left alone. If a child approaches you with something difficult, then you deal with it. But you don't keep conjuring it up. I understand that Felice would go to any length to make our classroom safe, and if the children needed to talk about scary things, they could. I appreciate the value of her way and respect her need to continue these talks, so I decided to sit down on the rug and participate in these conversations. However, when asked if I would have these kinds of discussions in my own classroom, I replied, "I don't think so. I still believe if a child speaks on it, I will address it. If the child does not say anything else about it, I feel the child has gotten everything he or she can from me." To my way of thinking, children should always be told if they have any questions or if there was anything else, they could speak about it. But I would not address it first.

FELICE: I felt the same way as Mrs. Reaves about these conversations at the beginning of my work with New Beginnings. I, like Mrs. Reaves, grew up in an environment in which my family didn't discuss issues that were troublesome and uncomfortable. Children weren't given the opportunity to express themselves. However, I realize now that there could be great benefit in these kinds of conversations. With so many emotionally needy children depending on me, the least I can do is to provide a safe, loving place where they have the freedom to talk about anything that is on their minds. I may not have all of the answers to their questions, nor can I solve their problems. I just have a rug with 26 friends who listen to their voices.

MARY: I definitely helped facilitate the development of Felice's relationships with our students' parents. At the beginning of the school year, parents would come into the classroom and walk right by Felice to talk to me. She sensed that the parents didn't like her because she was White. In fact, I often discouraged Felice from interacting with the parents so that I could take care of things. Although I knew she was an exceptionally strong and talented teacher, her fragile appearance and shy manner made me want to protect her. I know that when some African-American parents feel a White teacher is vulnerable, they may begin to find fault. At our first open house, my fear proved to be correct.

Open house occurs during October. Parents are invited to come into the classroom during the evening to meet the teacher. The teacher gives a brief talk about her plans for the school year. When Felice began her discussion with the parents that night, she was bombarded with questions and concerns. Many parents said, "Hmmm . . . no workbooks." "They learn through play? When are you going to teach reading and math?" "When he was in preschool, he was doing real work . . . he's too advanced to play all day." As the parents' voices grew louder, I left the room briefly, came back in, and sat down on the carpet. While Felice was addressing the parents, I interjected and elaborated on her points. I wanted to send the message that she was competent and that I respected her. Later, when Felice asked me about this, I said, "When I heard what was happening, I returned to the room immediately because had I been in an all-White situation, I would want someone to have my back." I was not prepared to leave her out there like that. I remember sitting up with her telling the parents, "No, this is what we do—she does it this way. I see nothing wrong with it. Your son needs to learn how to do this. He will benefit." Then everyone was OK with Mrs. Wagman.

FELICE: As the year went by, if parents still had questions or concerns, they would continue to go to Mrs. Reaves first. Mrs. Reaves was worried that I would have a problem with that. I guess I was a little jealous. However, I was glad she stepped in and helped me. Mrs. Reaves understood the parents better than I did.

MARY: By interceding with the parents, I was not trying to overshadow Felice in any way. It's just that they felt more comfortable coming to me. I am an older Black woman and they are young. They come to me because I am like their mother or grandmother and they feel they can relate to me better.

FELICE: It was only during a telephone conversation the following summer that I learned from Mrs. Reaves that the parents respected my work. I didn't know about all of the conversations she was having with the parents throughout the year. She would talk to parents—at the supermarket, on the street corner, at their houses, or even after school while I was standing a few feet away—and brag about all of the interesting things going on in our classroom.

MARY: I wanted the parents to know that when they saw Felice, they could not come in and do or say whatever they wanted. I would not allow that. Their kids loved her and when the children love you, you are doing something right. And it wasn't just for what she could give them; they truly loved her because she treated them like they were little individuals, as if they were her own children. I think that I succeeded in helping bridge a gap between Felice and the parents.

FELICE: It was my intention to keep a low profile and concentrate on my teaching. It was my relationship with Mrs. Reaves and, in turn, her relationship with the staff that changed this dynamic. I was especially glad that she introduced me to Mrs. Banks, a vocal and influential aide at Clinton. At Mrs. Reaves's prodding, Mrs. Banks came into my room one day. Mrs. Banks said, "I want to see what all the fuss is about in this room. I heard a lot about this class." I was scared. Everyone sat down on the rug and the day began. We were talking about mothers in the morning meeting. Many of the children spoke: "My mommy works at Pathmark." "My mother can drive me to school." "I sleep with my mother in the bed and she can read to me." Then it was Mrs. Banks's turn. She said something like, "Mothers fix children's dinner and hug them before putting them to bed." We wrote down her words along with the children's on chart paper. Later on in the week, she came back to visit our class. She saw that we had hung the chart up on a bulletin board. She smiled. If Mrs. Banks likes you, than everyone likes you. It was then that I knew she liked me.

MARY: Felice left Clinton at the end of April to have her baby and to spend time raising her. It doesn't surprise me that months later our former students still come by to ask me about her and the baby. I think it's because she always listened to them and valued what they had to say. I looked forward to our morning meetings. It's amazing to hear 5- and 6-year-olds discuss topics like what to do if someone knocks down your block building, death, monsters, guns, and what babies do when they're inside their mother's body. Felice taught me that children have ideas and it's important that we give them the opportunity to express them.

I helped plan Felice's baby shower at the end of April. I wanted it to be special, so I made sure everyone came and brought nice presents. In truth, people wanted to be there. They really liked her! We soon found out that when she added a little bass to her voice, she's a wonderful teacher and someone I'd be happy to call my daughter.

FELICE: The realization that I became an insider at Clinton Avenue occurred at my baby shower. Teachers, aides, parents, and even the security guard all showed up to surprise me. The most moving part of it all was Mrs. Banks's gift. A few days earlier, she had asked me if I would like to have an old family heirloom. She wanted to give me a cradle in which all of her children had slept. I replied that I would be honored. When her son brought it to school freshly painted, complete with a sheet, pillow, and a new comforter, I started to cry. Imagine—my newly born Caucasian baby would be sleeping in the same cradle that had rocked Mrs. Banks's newborn African-American babies to sleep. What a beautiful thing!

13

On the Bridge That We
Are Building

MARGOT HAMMOND WITH MARVA WRIGHT BANKS,
ETHEL M. COTTEN, EVANGELINE DENT, MARY REAVES

New Beginnings staff developer Margot Hammond cannot make sense of the direct, often "harsh" forms of discipline that she witnesses among African-American paraprofessionals and their deep caring for the children of Newark. At the same time, she recognizes that all of her own well-intentioned talk is of little use. This chapter documents Hammond's efforts to understand the situation in which she finds herself through regular meetings with coauthors Marva Banks, Ethel Cotten, Evangeline Dent, and Mary Reaves. Hammond's action research leads to surprising changes for the paraprofessionals and herself.

THE TEACHERS' LOUNGE at Clinton Avenue Elementary School is small and cozy. There is just enough space in the center of the room for a table and six chairs. A soda machine sits at one end and a sink at the other. The microwave is close by. Even though everyone complains about the lack of comfort, almost every day a group of paraprofessionals gathers together to eat lunch. Topics for conversation include school gossip, family news, and district and state education policy. Laughter abounds and loud enthusiastic voices can usually be heard echoing off the cinder-block walls.

It was at lunch one day, during my first year as a staff developer at the school, while listening to the paraprofessionals, that I first realized how concerned they were about the children. Mary, Marva, Ethel, and Evangeline were talking about a child who was going into foster care and the struggles of her family with drugs and jail. I was drawn to them, eager to learn more about what each one knew of the community and teaching in Newark.

FIRST IMPRESSIONS

I met Mary Reaves first, when I entered one of the kindergarten rooms, looking for the teacher I'd been sent to mentor. Instead of the teacher, I found Ms. Reaves. Her manner was calm and firm, and I could see from her expression that she really liked the children. It was time for the morning meeting—coming together to sing, review the calendar, and record the weather. The children were restless. Ms. Reaves, patient, yet determined to proceed, reminded them to listen and settle down. After several minutes of this and with one child in desperate need of individual attention, she changed course abruptly. "Do you read to kids?" she asked me in an exasperated tone. When I said yes, Mary responded quickly, "Good. Then will you please read this to them, now?" and handed me a book.

I recently reminded Mary of this story and she laughed with appreciation. Tired of the upheaval that she and the rest of the school staff was feeling as a result of the state takeover, Mary says that she was glad anytime someone came to her room who could be of actual help. Down to earth, practical, with no pretensions, Mary likes to talk and is a good storyteller. Someone who takes the most difficult children under her wing, she can frequently be seen walking the school halls with a child or two in tow. Her own children are raised and grown. Although only in her early 50s, she has grandchildren now.

Right from the start, Ethel Cotten impressed me as someone who cares deeply about the well-being of both the children in her care and the teachers with whom she works. She speaks of children with genuine interest and understanding, focusing on their capabilities and strengths. She is proud of their accomplishments and sets high expectations for all the children with whom she works. Children are lucky to be in her class. And teachers are lucky to have her as an aide.

When I first met Ethel, she was working with Margaret, a teacher new to teaching and to Newark. Young, White, and progressive, Margaret was criticized by the Clinton staff for her lack of authority and her inability to discipline the children. But Ethel saw what Margaret did well and appreciated how hard she worked. Throughout that year, with concern and perseverance, but not much success, Ethel tried to help the struggling young teacher gain control of the class.

One day early in the spring, Margaret was out sick, and Ms. Cotten was in charge. She didn't smile a lot and had a firm grip on the classroom. There was less playing that day, more time sitting at attention, waiting for everyone to be ready. The children were calmer, and the noise level was lower. There was also less fighting. It was clear to me that Ms. Cotten was able to control the children, but unfortunately she was not able to help the rookie teacher do the same.

Marva Wright Banks, the community aide at the Clinton Avenue School, moves through the halls with a distinct majesty. She never hurries, and the deliberateness in her step and manner demands respect. I had heard that Marva did not care much for New Beginnings—neither our methods nor our staff developers.

We got to know each other, one short conversation at a time. About every 2 weeks, Marva would stop me in the hall to ask about our program. "What is all the playing for?" "Where are the ABC's?" "Why is there so much noise?" "When will the kids learn to read?" I answered her questions carefully, but what really helped Marva to understand how New Beginnings works was the time she spent in classrooms.

Then, Marva and I became friends. First, I invited myself to go along when Marva and Mary went out to pick up Italian hot dogs for lunch. Next, Marva invited me to go with her to the Palm Sunday service at Greater Abyssinian, the church she attends each Sunday morning. Deeply honored, but a little nervous about the appropriateness of what I'd wear and certain that people would notice, I spent a lot of time getting dressed and arrived just in time for the service. I was not nearly dressed up enough. When Marva introduced me, first to her sister and then to the congregation, I was greeted with warmth and respect. In addition to the sermon, there were numerous individual announcements and spiritual testaments. No one seemed to be in any hurry. Everyone sang, and most of the congregation danced to the gospel music with great enthusiasm and joy. At the end of the service, the children's choir, all dressed alike in starched, pressed navy blue and white, girls in dresses or skirts and blouses, boys in pants, shirts, and ties, marched around the church while parents and grandparents, aunts and uncles looked on proudly. Driving back to New York City, I was filled with a new understanding of the power of the African-American community, an uplifted spirit, and a sense of being connected to Marva.

I got to know Evangeline Dent in a social context. Our first contact was on the dance floor at the school holiday celebration. After dinner and more than a little wine, someone turned up the music and people started to dance. I noticed Evangeline right away and, relating to the way in which she moved, figured that we'd grown up in the same era. As I watched her dance the Lindy Hop—step, step, back step—with a smooth soulful rhythm and sweet sassy grace, I asked if I could join her. Surprised, but willing to try me out as a partner, Evangeline agreed. I think in the end she was pleased with how well we danced together. The smile on her face, the dreamy look in her eyes, and the snap in her fingers let me know how much Evangeline enjoys music.

During that first year I worked with the kindergarten teachers and Evangeline was an aide in the first grade, so we didn't spend any time together in classrooms. On one occasion, however, I encountered her in the hall with a group of rowdy children. They were making too much noise, jumping out of line, and bumping into each other. A fight erupted. Ms. Dent grabbed the culprits and stood them against the wall. With true frustration and anger in her voice, she hollered, "Why can't you behave? What is wrong with you?" Then she looked at me apologetically and with some embarrassment and said, "I don't know why they can't behave. I don't know what to do with them." In that moment I saw how worried Evangeline was about the children. Not only worried about how they behaved in school, but about how the children's out of control behavior looked to outsiders and could adversely affect the rest of their lives.

MY STORY AND THEIRS

When I began working in Newark, I was upset by what appeared to be severe and harsh treatment of children. In my opinion, there was too much yelling, too many negative interactions and not enough positive ones. I did not like what I saw, and siding with the children I felt angry at the administrators, teachers, and paraprofessionals.

I was assigned to Clinton in the midst of the project's second year. Conversations about social–emotional development were in progress. The school climate and discipline were already a part of the agenda, and the principal was calling for a "tone of decency."

I have worked for 25 years in independent, progressive schools whose cultures encourage children to question authority as a means to promoting independence, individuality, and autonomy. In all of these settings, within a carefully planned structure, children are given a great deal of freedom and choice. Teachers routinely explain reasons for limits, stress fairness, and speak in quiet, calm tones. I wanted to try that—what I thought of as a kinder, more respectful approach—at Clinton. However, children responded to my kindness with disrespect, to my quiet tone of voice with increasingly louder voices of their own, and to my pleas for good behavior with uncontrolled wildness.

As a child I experienced firm, harsh, and sometimes severe discipline. I also experienced abuse. I spent a good deal of my young adulthood trying to tease apart the subtle and not so subtle differences between discipline and abuse, firmness and harshness, kindness and weakness. In Newark I was again faced with looking at these distinctions. This time around, however, I would be learning to read the exercise of authority and discipline as culturally determined practices.

I was seeing behavior that I had a difficulty understanding. Adults whom I liked were speaking to children in ways that seemed harsh and unnecessarily stern. The children in turn respected the teachers but did not respond to my own kind and "respectful" words. I decided to refrain from making judgments and to take a closer look at the interactions between the children and adults in the school, particularly the paraprofessionals. I planned to watch and listen carefully for differences in tone and language, within and across culture and race. I looked for the caring and concern in these interactions. I wanted to know more about what worked and why. My questions led me back to Mary, Marva, Ethel, and Evangeline. I knew that they had important knowledge that would help me to better understand the children, their families, and their culture.

During the spring semester of my third year in Newark, Mary, Marva, Ethel, Evangeline, and I met every 2 weeks. From early on it was evident that these four women had much in common. All are African-American, born between 1938 and 1949. Two were raised in the rural South, two in the urban North. Each has spent her adult life in the Newark area, raising children and working in the district schools for 20 to 30 years. They also share common values: family, friendship, community, and church.

Each time we came together, the interactions were energetic, emotional, joyful, and memorable. I asked them to talk about their childhoods—early schooling and communities—becoming a parent and paraprofessional, and their goals for children today. At the end of our first session, the tape ran out and I had to turn the recorder off, but all four participants kept right on talking, excited by the others' stories and their own. When I joked about how they wouldn't stop, one of them asserted proudly, "Nobody ever asked me to tell my story before, and I like telling it."

Authority and Discipline: At Home and At School

As children, the paraprofessionals reported that they were disciplined both at home and at school in a firm and sometimes harsh manner. This was true for many African-American children during the late 1940s and early 1950s, when adults still believed in corporal punishment. There was no doubt or debate about who was in charge. Adults made the rules and expected children to comply. Marva explained:

> We would get a whooping. It wasn't child abuse. It was discipline. I think we had a good life. My mother raised all of us. We learned values and morals that kids don't learn today, like to respect others if you want to be respected.

Today a "whooping" of any kind is considered child abuse by many, an offense that must be reported to children's services. A teacher can get fired for hitting a child. A parent can lose custody. While I was raised to expect a spanking whenever I transgressed, I do not believe in corporal punishment. As a young parent and educator, I was greatly influenced by my time at Bank Street College. Here I encountered a progressive approach to discipline, one that emphasizes learning self-control as an important first step in getting along with others. Listening to Marva, however, I came to agree that many of the children in Newark needed to show more respect. I wanted to understand more about why she and her fellow paraprofessionals believed that strict discipline, even a spanking, might achieve that goal.

There is a growing body of research on cultural differences in discipline practices. Janice Hale (1982) describes one such study comparing child-rearing practices used by African-American and White grandmothers. Hale validates Marva's experience and supports her cultural belief in corporal punishment. Comer and Poussaint (1975/1992) explain:

> Under harsh social conditions of the past many African-American parents felt that they had to force their children to obey so that they would not violate any of the racial rules and bring harm to their families. This led some families to establish many hard and fast rules with severe punishment for even minor disobedience. (p. 52)

It is not hard to understand why African-American parents want their children to behave respectfully and to obey without delay. Historically, the world has been and continues to be a dangerous place for African-American children. Recently, a colleague, an African-American mother, helped me to understand this more fully, commenting, "Many

African-American mothers would say, 'It is better for me to spank my children as a way of preventing others from beating them. At least then I am in control of how hard they are being hit.'"

Hale (1982) suggests that African-American children often do not regard threats and reprimands as harshly as White teachers do, and that sometimes they experience them as bordering on play. On some occasions, as I watch a member of the Clinton community discipline a child, I notice how quiet the child becomes. Bowing in shame, looking respectfully at the adult, or nodding up and down in response to questions about improving behavior, the child indicates by body language a compliance and a willingness to do better. On other occasions, when the reprimand is sharp, filled with teasing and quick sting, I frequently see the child smile, shrug off the teasing, and move on.

When the paraprofessionals were growing up, parents widely accepted such stern disciplinary practices. Mary Reaves lived with her grandmother and parents on a farm in South Carolina. Here her family held teachers in high esteem and freely delegated the authority to discipline children.

> In the South, where I came from, even if you felt that the teacher was being mean to you, you still couldn't go home and complain to anyone because parents believed that teachers were gold upon the earth. You know, whatever the teacher said, that's the way it was.

Evangeline grew up and went to school in Elizabeth, New Jersey, and her experience was similar to Mary's.

> The relationship my mother had with the teachers—it was good. She told us to obey the teacher, listen and learn all you can. If you don't, she will discipline you. You did not disrespect the teacher.

Lines of authority were clear. Referring to the late 1940s and early 1950s when Mary was in school, Comer and Poussaint (1975/1992) write, "Principals and teachers together could establish and reinforce desirable student behavior. Most parents, students, and teachers accepted absolute principal and *teacher* power as the way things were and should be" (p. 5).

The benefit of such absolute authority and power was well-defined expectations. Parents generally reinforced the behavior and academic expectations, rewards, and punishments of the school. Violence and disrespect for authority figures were not tolerated. Marva comments:

We had to respect everybody. The principal said, "If you fight in the summer, you will get suspended in September." So people didn't really fight—nothing like that. You know, you had to respect grown people. And teachers—parents used to put them on a pedestal! We had to respect teachers because our mothers respected teachers.

I can appreciate why Marva might long for the days when parents set the rules and children followed, when schools were orderly and safe, when teachers and principals were truly in charge, and when parents uniformly supported school policy. By comparison, many of today's homes and schools are places of disorder and disrespect. But the good old days were not all good. Sometimes parents went too far and the deliberate, controlled use of a switch turned into a violent beating. Teachers and school administrators were known to abuse their power (Comer & Poussaint, 1975/1992).

In our conversations, Mary, Marva, Ethel, Evangeline, and I often reached a juncture where my progressive values such as autonomy, self-expression, and independence clashed with their more traditional African-American values. At moments like this, I recalled the words of my African-American colleague about how many African-American parents believe that schools should "Teach the children to behave and be respectful of authority, no matter what, so they don't get into trouble. If you are an African-American child and you get into trouble, you can end up dead."

Life is certainly more complicated today than it was in the 1950s. School problems with regard to authority, respect, and discipline reflect problems in communities, in families, and in our larger society. There are no easy answers or universal solutions. Listening to the Clinton paraprofessionals, I realize that there is a range of possible ways to discipline children, many that can be characterized as firm and strict but also fair and humane. I know too that I have changed the way I discipline the kids at Clinton. I feel Mary, Marva, Ethel, and Evangeline's influence every time I stare silently to command respect, or snap my fingers and point to indicate quickly where I need a child to move.

Parental and Community Involvement: Then and Now

As children, the paraprofessionals lived in families and communities where the adults were actively involved in their lives. Adults not only took care of their own children but also looked out for each other's. They placed a high value on education and took an interest in their children's schooling. Ethel was a "country girl." She grew up on a farm in North Carolina and was the youngest of 10.

> I had to ride the bus to school and my brother was the bus driver. So I would take the bus to school every day and kids would say, "Oh, here comes the country girl." But my dad had this farm and so when I was 12, the kids from my school came out to our farm and dad taught them how to make molasses. So then, after that, I was everyone's friend.
> My parents were very involved in our school. They had a tutoring program after school, and my dad was a volunteer in that program. When he could, he would come to the school to give help to the children who needed one-on-one.

Marva grew up in Newark, one of 12 children. Her father died when she was a little girl, and her mother raised the children on her own.

> Yeah, I guess I lived in the ghetto. I never knew it. We lived on Charles Street, and everyone was one big family. It was a one-way street, and everybody knew everybody from one end of the street to the other. It was just like our own little village there. And we ran in and out of each other's houses.

As young parents, raising children in Newark during the 1960s, the paraprofessionals, like their parents and grandparents before them, not only cared for their own children but also looked after the neighborhood kids. As parent volunteers, they became actively involved in their children's schools. As Evangeline explains, that kind of involvement is much rarer today:

> Both parents are working now. And they don't have time to come to school to see what is going on. We were at home more. We were able to get up to the school to see what our kids were doing, how the teachers were doing, how the schools were educating them.

Today, only a few parents from the Clinton Avenue community are actively involved in the school. The paraprofessionals are deeply concerned about this, and Mary offers the following explanation:

The exodus from the city to the suburbs started and then, most likely, with the poor economy and unemployment rates being high, parents lost hope, so some turned to drugs. Once they started using drugs, then the focus was not on the children. The focus was on "Where can I get my next hit?" I'm not saying that's what happened to everyone, but here in the inner city, some felt powerless. They couldn't get jobs. Many of them did not finish high school because they got caught up in the drug scene.

Parents fear losing their jobs because they know that is the only source of income they have. When you think of a mother being the head of the household, she is only one check away from poverty. So she has to weigh her job survival against going to see about her kids at school.

The paraprofessionals provide an important link to the community in which the children live. Parents trust them, take direction from them, and, in some cases, were even taught by them. The obstacles the paraprofessionals describe as reasons for lack of parental involvement are daunting. However, along with Marva, Ethel, Mary, and Evangeline, I believe that parental involvement is a critical component of school success. If we look to their experiences as young parents as a model for successful parent involvement, as well as for the professionalization of parents in schools, then perhaps we can feel more hopeful.

Head Start as a Model for Parent Empowerment and Professional Development

In an effort to learn more about the history of the professionalization of parents in poor neighborhoods, I also looked at the literature on Head Start (Ellsworth & Ames, 1998). The 1960s and 1970s were exciting times for parents in poor urban school districts. The War on Poverty was in full swing. Programs to address the lack of equity in education and employment had taken root, and there was a growing sense of possibility. Head Start, with its emphasis on involving parents, was one of the most important and successful of these programs.

The original Head Start proposal, entitled "Improving the Opportunities and Achievements of the Children of the Poor," recommended a wide range of parent activities in center programming. These included acquainting other residents with Head Start services; helping center staff understand the neighborhood; learning parenting skills; and supervising the children of other parents who are participating in center activities. It also noted that parents could fill a variety of nonprofessional and semiprofessional roles, as necessary for operating the center.

In the 1970s, Mary and Evangeline were hired as part-time, noninstructional aides. Both had dreamed of being teachers, but circumstances prevented them from realizing their dreams. As young mothers, Ethel and Marva became active in their children's schools, worked as volunteers, and were eventually hired as teacher aides. Ethel's work in her daughter's parochial school developed gradually but, as is often the case with very helpful volunteers, she became indispensable.

> In '65 I volunteered as a mother at the school, reading with the kindergarten. From there I got involved with the Mother's Club, became the president of the Mother's Club. Then I started coming at lunchtime, reading, volunteering. And one of the nuns said, "Why don't you just try to get permanent?" They had Title I then, so I went down, applied, and was hired.

Given Marva's deep commitment to the importance of parental involvement and her belief that parents have the power to change schools, it does not surprise me that she began her own involvement with Newark's school district as a Head Start parent.

> I think it was around '65 when my baby was in Head Start. I started out in South 17th Street School during the summer, doing the Head Start programs. I was a volunteer parent because my baby was only 5, and when your baby is 5 you follow her into school.

As the Head Start program developed, ideas about how best to involve parents expanded to include a role as decision makers on Head Start policy boards. Parents believed that they had the power to make schools work for their children (Pizzo, 1993). As a group the Clinton paraprofessionals were energized by Head Start. When their children reached school age, they continued to be active participants in the educational process. Each time they spoke about their early involvement in the schools, it was with enthusiasm and a sense of commitment and pride. Marva comments:

> In '69 we [a group of parents] were instrumental in getting this building built [Clinton Avenue School] quickly. I used to take a group of kids and march around the school outside and tell the men to get to work and build our school.

Mary adds:

> When I first started here, parents were a big part of the school, like
> what we are trying to get back to now. You did nothing without
> the parents being involved, and if they did not like something that
> was going down, the parents let the school know. I mean I have
> seen parents put principals out of the schools. So they had power
> and a lot of them were very political too.

According to Jean Anyon (1997), there were significant problems
in Newark's schools during the 1970s. Involved parents, like Marva,
Mary, Evangeline, and Ethel, were an important part of the call for
change during that era.

Unfortunately, what happened in Newark as parents gained power
in schools happened elsewhere. Emboldened by their Head Start experiences, they pushed at the doors of the public schools only to find them
slammed in their faces (Ellsworth & Ames, 1998). Marva explains how
school officials coopted parents as a means of quieting them:

> At that time, in the '70s, parents were so vocal and so powerful,
> that they could get things done. So someone sat down some-
> where and said, "We are going to take all of those powerful
> parents at Clinton Avenue and we're going to give them jobs.
> That way they can't go against the school system."

Through our conversations, the pivotal role that Head Start played
in the personal and professional lives of the paraprofessionals became
more evident. The Head Start experience deepened their commitment
to parent involvement, fueled their optimism about change, and confirmed a sense of personal efficacy.

COMING TOGETHER: WHAT WE WANT FOR CHILDREN

As the paraprofessionals and I learned about each other's lives and shared
our ideas, we moved toward each other on the bridge that we continue
to build. They enabled me to walk in a different world from the one in
which I grew up and lived. We were separated by race, ethnicity, geography, and income levels, but some of what we experienced in school
and at home—tough teachers, strict discipline, corporal punishment—
was the same. As a young teacher and mother, I first encountered and
then embraced a progressive approach. For most of their professional

lives, these paraprofessionals stayed committed to what they had known as children, a traditional approach to education and discipline.

Through our conversations and shared experiences at Clinton, we are building a bridge to change. For my part, I have learned to observe and listen without judging. I have come to a better understanding and acceptance of the ways in which Marva, Mary, Ethel, and Evangeline think about authority and discipline. I value their commitment to family and community. I am moved by their activism and optimism about the power of parents to do good.

The paraprofessionals have also changed. What these women want for the children they have raised and for the children they teach illustrates the steps they have taken toward a more progressive way of thinking and doing. In our final conversation, they talked about their current educational commitments:

- *Learning should be active, experiential, and focused on the child.*
  I think New Beginnings has gotten us to focus more on the child. Before it was about where this child should be and not about what this child needed to get to that point. By focusing on the child, it has made us all take a step back and look. It is about developmental needs and the child.—*Mary*

- *Skill work should be imbedded in interesting age-appropriate content.*
  We also know that playing with blocks is not just play. It's learning. A child might discover that this block is shorter than that one, that this one is longer, and how many of these little blocks it would take to make one of the big ones. All of these things help develop his mind. He is investigating things on his own.—*Mary*

- *Healthy social-emotional development is central to the learning process.*
  I think you have to let the children know that they are important and they are special. I think children should be allowed to express themselves. Don't be afraid to talk. Don't be afraid to be active in any subject in the classroom.—*Ethel*

- *Building good relationships between children and teachers and teachers and families is central to the learning process.*
  We are the foundation, and I want all the kids to succeed, be successful in life. All the kids who need help, I hope we can get it for them now, while they are still small. We need to see

what we can do for them, getting them through some bad times. My grandkids, I want the same thing for them. We have to get to the parents to let them know, we need parental involvement.—*Marva*

As school reformers, it's not enough for us to go into schools to share our ideas with people and hope that change will occur spontaneously. We can't count on people to adopt our ideas, even though they may be educationally sound and research-based. The real change, the kind that lasts, happens when people come together, learn from each other, and change in the process. That is what happened for me and the paraprofessionals at Clinton Avenue. We all changed.

As a part of a New Beginnings course, Marva and the other paraprofessionals were involved in constructing a developmental framework for 5- and 6-year-old children. They used their own observations of children as a starting point and added what they had read to round out the picture. When a school-wide meeting several weeks later gave them an opportunity to use the framework they had created, these four women were the first to bring their work to the table. The image of each of them eagerly retrieving and sharing their framework was visible proof of how they are learning to participate in the school reform conversation with better informed and more confident voices.

14

What Counts for Caring?

JUDITH W. LESCH

Judy Lesch, a member of the Bank Street Graduate Faculty and a New Beginnings staff developer, reflects on her work with African-American teachers in Newark. Through a close reading of the literature by African-American feminists, Lesch deconstructs her class- and race-based assumptions about choice and individual agency as well as her failure to understand the communicative styles of the women with whom she worked. This essay is testimony to the distances that must sometimes be spanned in order to build effective relationships in school change projects.

I T IS MY FIRST DAY as a staff developer at Mercer Avenue School, and I have spent time with three teachers in their classrooms. Now Aleisha* stands close to me at the end of the day as all the children are getting ready to go home.

"You married?" she asks.

"Yes."

"You married to a Black man?"

"No."

"You married to someone your color?"

"Yes."

Aleisha is 4, one of the youngest in this kindergarten class. She stands sturdily in a washed, loose, cotton dress, lots of pigtails in her hair. It is hard for her to listen too long in the group. We spent some

---

*All names are pseudonyms.

time together around her painting this afternoon. She layered her colors one on top of the other in a horizontal swatch, each new stroke achieving a new color and a thicker effect. Now we are beginning a kind of friendship; she knows I will be back on Thursdays.

The fact of my presence and my outsider status is as obvious as the color of my hair to Aleisha. She is not "color-blind" and she notices differences in her environment. It was with a sense of uncertainty that I acknowledged my White identity to Aleisha in this brief conversation. I sensed and hoped that she wanted to claim me as belonging to what she knew. I wanted her teachers and others in her community to accept me in a similar way, as someone who could share their common purpose of improving education for children in Newark. Aleisha was a curious researcher of her world, attempting to understand my identity and presence in her school. Did I bring the same quest for understanding to her community, and to the teachers in her life?

In this chapter I want to explore my experience as a White outsider providing staff development to African-American teachers serving a predominately African-American community. I entered this work with the belief that I could form strong relationships with anyone around "teacher issues"—issues focused on children's needs, ways of learning, and the organization of curriculum and materials. I believed then and I do now that teachers and staff developers from very different backgrounds can work together effectively. But my initial conversation with Aleisha proved unusual; issues of race as well as issues of class and culture were rarely discussed either during my visits to Newark or back home in New Beginnings staff meetings.

All ideas about teaching are situated in particular social, political, and historical contexts. My work in Newark has made me realize how important it is to become aware of the assumptions and values that underlie our understandings of best educational practices. Effective staff development occurs when staff developers are willing to make their beliefs explicit and engage in conversations with teachers whose values and understandings may be very different from their own.

During the 2 years I worked at Mercer School, I was filled with an overwhelming sense of confusion, of being unable to see and understand what was going on, of missing signals and meanings, of not grasping the context and life experiences of those around me. Over the following years, no longer a part of New Beginnings, I revisited my experience in Newark again and again, through memory, writing, and readings in African-American studies. I began to consider more carefully the material forces that shaped the consciousness of the teachers as well as my own. Although we shared common experiences as women, these were complicated by race and class identities, sometimes shared and sometimes not. What follows is my reconsideration of the ways different cultural meanings can be constructed around staff development work and educational practice.

EDUCATING 5-YEAR-OLDS

During the time I worked at Mercer School, I regularly visited other kindergarten classrooms across the river in New York City and its suburbs, as part of my work as an advisor at Bank Street College. In many of these classrooms, which had a mostly White, middle-class population, the children sat on the rug in a circle for an extended morning meeting that featured discussion among the children. The expectation in these classes was that children would express their ideas verbally, take turns and listen to each other, and independently carry out their designated roles for the day, such as calendar or daily schedule. Children talked to each other a lot in these classrooms, and the teacher's role was to remind them of the rules of listening to one another and to facilitate an orderly exchange of ideas.

At Mercer School I was the staff developer in the kindergarten classroom of Ms. Carter, an African-American teacher who had been selected to participate in New Beginnings and whose practices were based on her past experiences in the Newark Public Schools. In Ms. Carter's classroom, the children sat in assigned seats at the new tables that had recently replaced individual desks. Ms. Carter wanted the children to pay attention to her, to raise their hands to speak, and to focus on the important academic work of schooling that lay ahead of them. Ms. Carter was a commanding presence in the classroom, and she also had a warm and inviting quality. The children knew they were lucky to be in her class; they knew what she expected because she told them clearly and forcefully from the start.

In both Newark and New York, kindergarten children were learning the rules of school, in particular that they would be expected to sit and listen for long periods of time. But there were clear differences in what each group was learning, and those differences extended throughout the school day. In the New York classrooms in which I observed, the children made choices among activities, and children were encouraged to figure out problems—both academic and social—on their own. In the beginning of the school year, Ms. Carter told the children in her classroom what they needed to know, often as they were sitting at their tables or in a group on the rug. They were given specific learning tasks to accomplish, and Ms. Carter dealt quickly and authoritatively with social conflicts among the children.

STAFF DEVELOPMENT: CHALLENGES

As I started my work, I saw my job as helping Ms. Carter to change her approach to teaching so that it was more reflective of developmentally appropriate practices (Bredekamp & Copple, 1997; Williams, 1999). Although acknowledging the critiques of developmentally appropriate practice over the last decades (Delpit, 1986; New, 1994; Meier, 1999; Phillips, 1994), I held the basic tenets of this approach as fundamental to my vision of early childhood education.

Ms. Carter was beginning a transition from the more traditional educational methods used formerly at Mercer to the kind of learning environment proposed by the New Beginnings summer workshop she had just attended. I felt a great responsibility to be in the role of helping her make this change. Although I anticipated initial resistance, I was confident that Ms. Carter and the other teachers would eventually see the New Beginnings methodology as powerful and liberating for themselves and for the children. I wanted the children of Newark, especially those who were growing up in poverty, to have the same kind of classroom experience that I saw in those middle-class kindergartens across the river.

In Dewey's words, "What the best and wisest parent wants for his own child, that must the community want for all its children" (Dewey, 1900/1956). The problem was that I held an implicit assumption that "the best and wisest parent" was a universal version of a parent who looked like me. My vision of an appropriate early childhood classroom was an unchanging image of practices that could be transferred to any setting with only minor adjustment. I thought the challenge was to help Ms. Carter and the other teachers introduce these new approaches into their classrooms. I realize now that I had another challenge before me: to understand the different forms that exemplary early childhood practice takes in different settings.

Arriving on the scene shortly after the state takeover of the Newark Public Schools, New Beginnings entered a district that had suffered years of neglect and mismanagement (see chap. 5). It seemed to me that teachers received most of the blame for the failures of public education and most of the responsibility for applying shifting "remedies." Consequently, many teachers were focused only on what "had to be done" for the principal, the superintendent, and the state regulators. As another teacher in the school said wearily to me, the newest in a string of outsiders who had been brought in to "fix" her teaching, "Just tell me what to do and I'll do it."

My understanding of good educational practice could not be so easily translated into a checklist of "things to do." My goal as a staff developer was first to establish a trusting, respectful relationship with each teacher. On the basis of past experience, I believed that the best staff development occurs when a group of teachers come together to share their practice in a collaborative manner. I envisioned our meetings as conversations about new ways to do things in the classroom, focused in the beginning on a few simple alternatives to the traditional methods used by most teachers. I wanted the teachers to come to trust me, to know me as someone open and warm, accepting of others, nonjudgmental, able to listen and to communicate my ideas effectively.

The reality, as always, was more complex. Although my goals for the teachers were clear to me, and I understood that change is a slow process, I grew increasingly frustrated at how little seemed to get accomplished from one visit to the next. Ms. Carter and the other teachers had to revisit many district-based problems, which I had no power to change. But I couldn't seem to address the issues that were uppermost in my mind, such as how to help the children engage independently in different learning activities. Because I wanted to show my support for the teachers, I hesitated to give them specific directions for changing their reaching. Instead, I tried to model new approaches in their classrooms and to make indirect suggestions about classroom practices that were consonant with the project's goals.

Ms. Carter was an especially articulate speaker whose words and sentences flowed seamlessly. In fact, she was very effective when she explained the purposes of New Beginnings to community members and other teachers. Yet my suggestions and modeling about ways to give more autonomy to the kindergartners in her classroom seemed to have little impact in the beginning.

In an attempt to be collaborative, I often asked Ms. Carter to direct *me* in how to help her become a better teacher. Ms. Carter knew what she wanted: more teaching materials and help dealing with the conflicting expectations from New Beginnings and the school district. But the issues of pedagogy and the shared conversations about teaching practices I had envisioned having with her seemed to drift away.

As time went on, Ms. Carter did make many changes in her ways of working with the children in her classroom. But I left Newark after 2 years with a sense of confusion about the staff development process and my own understanding of the core elements of early childhood education. These questions led me back to my own initial expectations for the partnerships I had undertaken.

PERSPECTIVES AND ASSUMPTIONS

I came to Newark believing that my past experiences and commitment to equity would make me sensitive to issues of class and race as well as to the particular forms of discrimination that may have been experienced by African Americans living in Newark (see chaps. 1 and 6). In the midwestern, White, middle-class household of my childhood, social justice and racial equality were strongly held values. I have many years of experience teaching children from different racial, cultural, and linguistic backgrounds. As an educator I worked hard to include families and to acknowledge their perspectives, understandings, and expectations of their children. During several summers, I had worked as one of the only Whites in an inner-city arts program in an African-American neighborhood. That experience had given me a sense of the richness and variety of one African-American community at the same time that I was experiencing the unfamiliar situation of being an outsider.

What did I and what did the African-American teachers bring to the New Beginnings partnership? In retrospect, I have become aware of how little I knew about their histories and about the complexities of their lived experiences. After I left Newark I attempted to learn about the broader, collective African-American heritage that can influence educational beliefs and communicative practices. There were undoubtedly many similarities and differences, cultural and noncultural, between me and the teachers with whom I worked. In the absence of long-term relationships, I at least wanted to educate myself about the varying perspectives that might emerge from different cultural and historical experiences.

Hecht, Collier, and Ribeau (1993) describe all culture as historically and ethnically emergent, always in the process of being cocreated, maintained, and changed by its members. Parham, White, and Ajamu (1999) suggest that African-American identity is expressed through a set of core beliefs and understandings that have served to buffer the effects of racism and oppression. In general terms, African Americans have been able to maintain a communal space through beliefs in assertiveness, interdependence, and collectivism, a sense of uniqueness and individual style, a focus on positivity and emotionality, and an appreciation of "realness" and direct experience. This communal space provides a "sense of worth, dignity, affiliation, and mutual support"

(p. 14). African Americans have needed to envision themselves in ways that are unaffected by the discrimination that has used race as a justification for inequality; but at the same time they have had to pay close attention to how they are seen by the dominant majority. This conflict has created the need for a "double-consciousness," in which African Americans perceive the world first in terms of their own reality and second in terms of how the larger society views them (DuBois, 1903/1993; Fordham, 1996; Ogbu, 1999; Scheurich, 1993).

In contrast, studies have shown that European Americans identify themselves as members of a unified culture, even when they belong to overlapping cultural groups. Some writers suggest that the core values of White European-American culture include a focus on individuality and independence, belief in equality, competition, and future orientation, a sense of practicality, and a striving toward self-actualization (Greenfield, 1994; Lynch & Hanson, 1998). Many authors have examined the ways these European-American values have obtained a normative status in our society, working in unacknowledged ways to maintain power and economic privilege (Fine, Weis, Powell, & Wong, 1997; Kalyanpur & Harry, 1999). Even though I was aware of the notion of "White privilege" before going to Newark, I am struck now by how difficult it was for me to incorporate this idea in my work (McIntosh, 1989).

REVISITING COMMUNICATION AND RELATIONSHIPS

All communication takes place within a cultural framework. Conversation and relationship are key factors in creating and maintaining cultural identity, and the salient features of the communication system help define the core symbols of an ethnic group. One of my unexamined assumptions as a staff developer had been that the teachers at Mercer School would understand me no matter how I communicated. Naively, I thought my style of communication reflected a shared code among teachers, and I didn't understand that my experiences of successful communication with other teachers, mostly White, was not normative. I had not considered that there might be differences in communication and style that characterized African-American conversation, nor had I thought about the possibility of adjusting my own style of communicating to fit a different pattern (Hecht et al., 1993).

I knew I was having trouble communicating my teaching ideas to Ms. Carter, but I continued to use the reserved, indirect style of conversation that was familiar to me. Ms. Carter, on the other hand, could shift between many different styles of conversation—with her African-American coworkers, with the children in her classroom, with parents, with the administration in her school, with me—and seemed able to communicate successfully with a wide range of people.

The literature suggests that an important component of successful intergroup communication for many African Americans is to accomplish a goal together, to attain a shared outcome (Hecht et al., 1993). When Ms. Carter made direct requests to me to solve some of the problems she faced with the district's expectations, I wonder if she was actually trying to set a concrete goal for us to accomplish together. Because the New Beginnings philosophy was not clearly translated into prescribed, sequential teaching objectives at this time, it may have been difficult for Ms. Carter to clarify the goals toward which we were working. In retrospect, I have come to understand that assertiveness and directness are valued in African-American communication and culture. My continued hesitation to take an assertive posture as a staff developer or to give Ms. Carter the opportunity to be assertive herself may have contributed to some of the misunderstanding between us (Lesch, 2000).

At one point during the year, I decided to try a more direct approach with Ms. Carter, partly in response to the inadequacy I was feeling in my role as a staff developer. I presented Ms. Carter with a written list of specific goals, changes I hoped she would make in her teaching practice. Ms. Carter's reaction to this list of goals was not positive, and she questioned strongly my right to require her compliance. I was surprised at her reaction, but looking back at this incident, I can see why she was upset.

Throughout our relationship I was unclear about the lines of authority with Ms. Carter. Was I truly a helpful "colleague," or was I someone who had supervisory power, who could evaluate the effectiveness of her work and make recommendations to others in the system? Ms. Carter raised these issues immediately when confronted with my written goals. I had been hired to change teaching practices, a role supported by the authorities in the school administration, yet I was presenting myself as a pleasant person who wanted to be helpful. This indirect and elliptical approach to our relationship must have been as confusing for her as it eventually was for me. By acting as though our relationship was an open, friendly interchange about teaching ideas and practices, I realize I may have been contributing to her sense of powerlessness.

The fact is, I did not want to think about my role as an authority with power over Ms. Carter, and I did not consider how she might have experienced my status as a White outsider. These issues were never discussed between us or among others during my years in Newark. In many ways my work with Ms. Carter and the other African-American teachers in the school may have been a replay of the power relationships that they had experienced in other venues. As Thompson (1998) remarks, being aware of power as revealed in relationships is especially difficult "for those of us who are privileged enough not to notice the workings of power in our day to day lives" (p. 528). I realize now that my indirect communication style could have been received as carrying hidden authority and unacknowledged power, which may have been especially troubling and demeaning to women who had experienced some aspects of powerlessness throughout their lives. I have come to see my silence about power and authority as standing in the way of my developing an authentic and trusting relationship with Ms. Carter.

EARLY CHILDHOOD EDUCATION

New Beginnings had been invited to Newark to change early childhood teaching practices. A constructivist philosophy infused our work—the belief that young children learn best through active engagement with ideas, materials, and real-life tasks. I wanted the children in Ms. Carter's classroom to choose among a rich array of materials and activities, to explore and question and imagine, to develop their individual interests and strengths. Early in the first year of our work together, Ms. Carter questioned whether this "child-centered" approach would prepare her students for the standardized tests in their futures—tests that required the children to know specific information, tests that would be used by the state to measure her school's improvement.

For all the teachers in Newark—White, Black, and Hispanic—raising children's academic performance was the overarching goal. But I wonder if many of the teachers also understood that the children in their classrooms would be victims of the racism that had limited human potential in their community for generations. I can imagine that for these teachers, the education of their children must have been a deadly serious business, suffused with the reality of their own experiences. The indirect methods of teaching and learning New Beginnings was promoting may have seemed too remote from the material the children were supposed to be learning for the state assessments looming ahead. What would be the substance of learning if it were left to the child to construct it from his or her own experience? How could children be expected to know information they had not been taught?

African-American women have often had to take on the role of keeper of knowledge, the wise experts who pass on to the younger generation "the understanding and strategies they need to survive racism" (Thompson, 1998). African-American teachers have often provided the unique Afrocentric communal space that nurtures self-esteem at the same time it negotiates the disjunction between home and school (Fordham, 1996; Ogbu, 1999; Parham et al., 1999). In Mercer School Ms. Carter had certainly played this role for many of the children and families in her class. I wondered what kind of role change I had been expecting of her. For women who are used to taking charge, moving from the role of dispenser of knowledge to one of "facilitator" not only counters a basic understanding of how learning occurs but also may serve to undermine their own sense of purpose, self-respect, and competence. In retrospect, I have come to see there are many different ways for even young children to learn, and best educational practices can and should use a variety of forms, with direct teaching being one of them (Cochran-Smith, 1995; Delpit, 1988; Ladson-Billings, 1994).

CARING AND THE INDIVIDUAL CHILD

A key component of the early childhood pedagogy I valued was the concept of "caring" based on the private nurturing—specifically, maternal relationships—portrayed by some feminists (Noddings, 1984; Shapiro & Nager, 1999). When I think about my life as a teacher, I realize how strongly my deepest instincts about teaching, caring, and nurturance are embedded in my own childhood experiences. These in turn entwine with what appeared to be the universality of the protected White middle-class world in which I grew up. My childhood, with a mother who made her home and children the center of her universe, embodied one view of a feminist caring perspective: the private-sphere values, the family unit as a haven from the surrounding community, the White female who had learned to be sensitive to the needs of others and to state those needs in indirect forms. I relived those values and patterns first as a mother to my own children and then again as a teacher, unconsciously gravitating to the kind of early childhood teaching that fit my beliefs and values. My image of caring and good schooling were inextricably woven together. In my interactions with children, I mirrored the indirect, relationship-based practice that sees a teacher's first responsibility as knowing and responding to each child as an individual.

I wonder if I fully understood the kinds of caring and nurturing available to children growing up in different African-American communities. According to Thompson (1998), for example, caring and nurturing may be seen as both a public and a private undertaking in many neighborhoods. The community at large, through extended and fictive kinship groups, through churches and community groups, has in the past often shared responsibility for children's well-being and nurturance (see chap. 1). In addition to their child-rearing responsibilities, African-American women have traditionally taken on prominent roles within their communities to promote social change and educational achievement. Private caring relationships with individual children are valued, preserved, and primary, but those relationships are also incorporated into the need to fight injustice in the interests of the larger African-American community. Thompson (1998) comments, "Love and caring do not step back from the world in order to return to innocence, but step out into the world in order to change it" (p. 533).

During my first months in Newark, I remember being uncomfortable with the authoritarian voices and directiveness used with children at Mercer School. I would cringe internally at those voices, which made me feel as if I were being scolded. I wondered about the impact on the children's self-esteem and willingness to take risks. As I watched Ms. Carter over time, however, I had to acknowledge the sense of comfort and safety that the children in her classroom experienced. She realized more clearly than I that the needs of individual children cannot be separated from the larger experiences and communication patterns of the classroom and community. Ms. Carter used the power of her voice to communicate authority, respect, and caring in ways that the children in her classroom and her community understood. Along with Thompson (1998), Ms. Carter taught me to ask, "What counts for caring?"

Let me be clear. I am not saying that appropriate practice for African-American children should be only authoritarian, teacher-directed, or group-centered. Rather, I am questioning my unthinking acceptance of a model that judges such practices as inferior or lacking in understanding. Good practice must take into account the multiple, socially constructed meanings of care within different cultures and communities, and the varied histories that underlie the authentic teaching voice within each of us.

If I want to work across race, culture, and class boundaries, I have to be responsible for seeing my actions, communication style, and assumptions about educational practice from the position of my White experience. I must be attentive to my tendency *not* to notice difference and therefore to universalize my own perspectives. In retrospect, I am learning that my unexplored experience as part of White culture can act as a screen to shield me from imagining different scenarios, interpretations, and ways to be an educator.

When I think back to my first year at Mercer, I remember the problems I had in communicating with Ms. Carter. But I also remember Ms. Carter's effective role as a community spokesperson for New Beginnings, even as she herself continued to question these new ideas. It is clear to me now that Ms. Carter brought to our work many different kinds of expertise about collective identity, learning, and communication across ethnic groups. Not all urban settings are the same, not all African Americans have similar beliefs about education and child rearing, and each school has its own culture. But as I continue to engage in this work, I will more fully comprehend the enormous complexity and appreciate the rich possibilities that differing life experiences have to offer the process of school change.

15

Public–Private Partnerships

Augusta Souza Kappner

*Gussie Kappner, president of Bank Street College, would be the first
to admit that she does not have the know-how to help teachers
change their classroom practices. She does know, though, how to
promote public–private partnerships between educational institutions. Kappner played a critical role in negotiating the first contract
between Bank Street and the Newark Public Schools and sustaining
the collaboration during a series of stressful events. She also reminds the reader that although there may have been initial differences in philosophy, the work of both partners is ultimately subject
to the same public demands for standards, accountability, and high-
stakes testing.*

I ARRIVED AT BANK STREET as the new president in July of 1995,
the same month the Newark Board of Education was disbanded.
Fresh from 2 years with the U.S. Department of Education (USDOE),
I was eager to return to the field from the heights of Washington, D.C.
Bank Street seemed an ideal place to work on issues of urban education
and the public good—an independent progressive school shielded from
the variable consequences of government funding.

In coming to Bank Street, I was acutely aware that I was joining an
institution that was much smaller than the public systems I had worked
in previously: USDOE and the City University of New York (CUNY). I
looked forward to working with large public systems again, but from a
different perspective. My new vantage point, I thought, would offer

greater flexibility and a better opportunity to maintain focus on a substantive approach. I looked forward to the ability to focus on the professional rather than the political needs of a system. I was also well aware that I was joining a highly specialized institution where the total work was education, more specifically, progressive education. Bank Street is progressive, private, and small—everything that traditional public school systems are not.

My choice to become involved with the Newark Public Schools corresponded to my perception of the mission and traditions of Bank Street, an institution that had been working in public school systems for close to 50 years. The proposed effort in Newark seemed to have a natural fit with the college's mission and approach (see chap. 2) and also provided me, as its new president, my first opportunity to work with Bank Street faculty and professional development staff in a project they would design with a public school system, create from the ground up, and then implement. Although I had heard much about Bank Street's work in the public schools, most of what I had observed firsthand was limited to Midtown West, a New York City public school that Bank Street had helped to launch, and Pittsburgh, where a Bank Street staff development project (Vision 21) was winding down after several years.

I knew well from my years of work in public systems the cost of "failure" in this situation—to the children, to the Newark staff, to the Bank Street staff, and to the reputation of the college. Whatever we did, it would be highly visible and would have strong implications for the credibility of the college in school reform efforts in other parts of the country. As the president of the institution, I was acutely attuned to this aspect of our work. As the newest member of the Bank Street team, I placed my trust in the faculty and staff that we could indeed meet the commitments being undertaken. I knew that as the college's president, I could encourage, I could support, I could envision, but that ultimately others—with the deep, more authentic knowledge of children, teachers, parents, and schools—would bring their talents to improving the schools.

Our specific relationship with Newark developed from an unusual mix of preparedness and serendipity. After the disbanding and takeover of the school district by the State of New Jersey, Dr. Beverly Hall was appointed by the New Jersey Commissioner of Education as the Newark superintendent. Dr. Hall had previously served as superintendent of District 27 in New York City, having risen through the ranks from teacher to principal to superintendent to deputy chancellor. I knew that Dr. Hall brought to her work a deep knowledge and commitment to early childhood education. She was familiar with Bank Street's approach to early childhood education and had experienced the Bank Street staff development process in New York. She knew firsthand about the work of several of the faculty and staff. She saw building a strong early-learning framework in the Newark Public Schools as critical to creating enduring change. She shared our thinking that however superb interventions at the upper grade levels might be, they were always regarded in some way as remedial, as attempts to fix something that was broken. Only through a more effective learning strategy in the early years could the system begin to look forward to youngsters' moving through the grades without remedial strategies but rather with enrichment strategies. Moreover, Dr. Hall understood that Bank Street's professional development approach was a long-term investment that would aid teachers—by building their professional capacity—long after Bank Street's involvement in the district ended.

This shared philosophy, and our personal mutual respect and trust, was critical to our decision at Bank Street to cross the river and make a major commitment to improving teaching and learning in the Newark Public Schools.

Working with large public systems is always a challenge. Newark, however, seemed small in comparison to New York City, where Bank Street was already working in hundreds of public schools—though granted not with the same intensity in most that we were ultimately to develop in Newark. Newark, by comparison, seemed conceptually manageable as a project—45,000 children, 4,500 teachers—as it could only to a lifelong New Yorker!

While big traditional public systems have their challenges, small, progressive private systems also have theirs. Moving between these two cultures and helping to bring them together in ways that worked productively for the children and teachers was sometimes the biggest challenge of all. For me, the greatest frustrations and tensions came from the multiple pressures on the Newark Public Schools. Even when the college and the Newark Public Schools clearly shared goals and objectives, these multiple pressures were ever present.

Having spent many years in large public systems myself, I often felt the frustration of knowing the common obstacles of bureaucracies. That is, I knew these structures couldn't be wished away, yet I still had to encourage the faculty and staff that, despite these obstacles, the work we were engaged in was having an impact on teachers and ultimately children.

In highly politicized public systems such as Newark, minor disagreements often escalate into major conflicts that prevent effective collaboration. In Newark, we all worked hard to prevent that from happening. Our efforts, I feel, were helped by the state-takeover status of the district; all the district's representatives and Bank Street's as well shared the same sense of urgency. We understood that all of our actions and their results were being watched carefully—by the state, the parents, and the Newark business community. We also understood that in this current standards-driven reform climate, the Newark Public Schools would ultimately be judged on a set of test scores, which, both partners agreed, were hardly an accurate reflection of the changes occurring for the children.

Not being a day-to-day player in Newark, I came to the table usually only when some issue—of program or funding—reached an impasse or absolutely needed the superintendent's and president's personal, professional attention. Otherwise, communication was by telephone and frequent. The Bank Street staff felt the pushes and pulls on a daily basis.

In times of transition or impasse, it was essential that I become more closely involved. During the life of the project, there have been changes in the positions of state superintendent of the Newark Public Schools and state commissioner of education. In both of these transitions, I initiated meetings with the new office holders to review the history of Bank Street in the Newark Public Schools, to discuss the Bank Street philosophy and approach, and to reaffirm our commitment to working with the Newark Public Schools. Developing a direct relationship with these state officials proved helpful later in coping with issues of budget. Commissioner Hespe was responsive and assigned state development staff to work with us on issues of funding.

I also advocated for our greater involvement in pre-K work statewide in New Jersey and initiated conversations about it with state early childhood administrators. My work with an early-childhood funders network in New York provided me with knowledge of early-childhood funding possibilities in New Jersey and the ability to connect the Newark project to these resources. This link to pre-K became increasingly important to the project as time went on.

As the business community became more interested in public education in Newark, we knew it would be critical for them to develop an understanding of Bank Street's work in the schools. At my request, a key business leader sponsored, in Newark, a dinner at which the business and funding community could meet a few Bank Street trustees and hear from the New Beginnings project director and the Newark superintendent about the goals, structure, and results of our work. This session, held in the administration of Beverly Hall, was helpful in gaining broader support for the project not only in Beverly Hall's administration but also after the transition to Marion Bolden's.

Part of a president's role in outreach projects is to communicate to both staff and community how much the institution values its relationship with the community. In-house at Bank Street I addressed this responsibility by including the New Beginnings project in president's reports to the college community and to the trustees, scheduling New Beginnings presentations to both staff and trustee audiences, and developing opportunities for New Beginnings to be publicized beyond Bank Street.

Within the Newark community, I set about accomplishing my role by attending key public events—and by inviting Newark Public Schools administrators and foundation representatives to New York to join Bank Street staff and trustees for an evening in my home to honor their work. In this social setting, individuals could talk comfortably with each other, begin to break down some of the rigidity of their respective roles, and share their mutual interest in improving the education of the children of Newark.

As the years progressed, several important developments occurred that were to affect teachers and others in the Newark Public Schools. First, aspects of particular approaches of the K–12 school reform movement became "institutionalized" through the passage by Congress of the Obey/Porter legislation tying Title I dollars to research-based school reform methodologies and the creation, with USDOE funding, of the whole school reform catalogue and its ancillary documents. This was occurring just as the *Abbott v. Burke* case was being settled, and these new rubrics, particularly Success for All, became favored state approaches to school reform. Districts and schools in New Jersey now had to select a state-approved school reform methodology to qualify for state funding.

Second, when Bank Street first began its work in the Newark Public Schools in 1996, only local foundations were funding school reform, but by 1998 the Ford Foundation was supporting a major implementation of Success for All in Newark. This confluence of state policy and new funding from a national foundation created the need for Bank Street to reach out to other program approaches that differed significantly in their philosophic bases and strategies, and to seek ways to work together. This was often difficult for Bank Street staff developers, who are extremely well grounded in the developmental-interaction approach and—like some of the whole school reform methodologists—wanted the opportunity to see the approach work in its purest form of implementation. It also meant that early lead funders had to reach out to later funders to discuss the relationship and impact of differing philanthropic strategies.

Finally, it meant that while attempting to maximize the available resources, the Newark Public Schools were now accountable to multiple funders.

Bank Street, as a small institution among much larger and better funded entities, had to think more clearly about its niche and its role relative to the many players now on the scene. As time went on, the project made several decisions that brought it closer to a whole school reform approach. It was decided to concentrate Bank Street's resources into fewer schools but more classrooms. Major components in family involvement, mental health, and leadership were added; and partnerships were developed with the Comer approach, the Accelerated Schools approach, the ALEM/Community of Learners approach, and the Coalition of Essential Schools. Expanding programming and partnerships was consistent with Bank Street's approach, which focuses on the whole child within his or her social context.

Working with the district, we also decided to expand into prekindergartens rather than into more third-grade classrooms. This reinforced our niche as a provider of early childhood learning staff development and the only provider of a constructivist, nonremedial basic teaching and learning strategy. It also allowed the district to pursue a test-preparation strategy that began to be felt only in the third grade. These decisions were made jointly over two administrations, first with Beverly Hall and later with her successor, Marion Bolden, and represented adaptations designed to meet the evolving needs expressed by the school system.

As president of a progressive institution in a markedly nonprogressive era, I have often spoken about the double burden we carry. If it is our intention to work with public schools, we must prepare teachers (or children, when we are in K–12 classrooms) in what we believe is the education everyone deserves. At the same time, we must demonstrate to systems that children prepared in this manner can meet the same rigorous grade-by-grade standards that form the core of K–12 reform in the year 2002. Newark tested our ability to meet these double performance standards. Although the verdict is still out on the future of the program, initial qualitative and quantitative evaluations indicate that children in New Beginnings classrooms have made both the test gains so easily understood by the general public and the more authentic educational and developmental gains valued by Bank Street.

In the end—and actually in the beginning and middle as well—this was for me the real challenge. The differences in cultures and ways of working between a large public system and a small independent system paled in comparison. These were predictable and not unlike difficulties presented by other situations in which I had participated. Because of the size and scope of the effort, the Newark project exposed a significant number of Bank Street staff to these intense differences in organizational culture, and these would now seem predictably familiar to them if we were beginning a similar project in a different city. But we still face the real challenge, both in Newark and beyond: How, confronting a system committed to extremely standardized test-driven reform strategies, does a progressive institution like Bank Street structure its staff development interventions to meet the needs of the children, the teachers and other professionals, and the school system while maintaining its integrity of philosophy and approach?

Should we simply refuse to work in situations in which we judge the other interventions to be incompatible with ours? This is the approach that Success for All has taken, holding out for being able to control all or at least most of the variables of implementation. Given the number of systems turning to test-driven reforms, this approach would dramatically limit the systems with which we could work. It would also restrict our opportunities to gather the kind of evidence about efficacy that politicians and publics expect in thinking about reform. Should we work to eliminate inappropriate tests? We did this in Newark, successfully eliminating a very poorly constructed kindergarten test—then found ourselves searching for new empirical data that would be valued by the state system and certain funders. Should we, as we pragmatically did in our work in Newark, make incremental decisions as we go along, negotiate compromises, and work collaboratively wherever possible? And does this in the end help the children and teachers more than our not being there?

What would I say to others about entering into such collaborations? I would be enthusiastically encouraging but clearly realistic. If there is strong initial trust between the leaders of the two institutions, it will go a long way in overcoming the organizational culture conflicts. It is important, if you wish to do this work, to be prepared to take risks around money and feel confident that your board of trustees would support this effort even if your decisions did not turn out well. In thinking about Bank Street's work in Newark, I am often reminded of the saying from the Greek historian Herodotus, "Great deeds are usually wrought at great risks." There is nothing neat about such projects; having the ability to live well with ambiguity will make it easier, as will having the fiscal flexibility to live with the often erratic payment schedules of large public systems. Throughout this type of endeavor, it is critical to continuously recognize and draw upon the strengths of the local partners and community. This will go far in responding to criticisms of your "outsider" status and in building a deep understanding among faculty and staff about the broader community context and aspirations.

Presidents are not able, in small institutions, to keep distance from such projects; be prepared to help out, to negotiate, and to threaten, as needed. Be prepared to keep your own staff's morale up in tough times. Insist on sufficient start-up time to build trust and relationships at all levels in the two institutions. We didn't have it in the first year. It took lots of backtracking to create it in the second year. Establish formal and informal communication systems through which you can head off crises and clarify messages to individuals through both organizations. And, learning from what we did not do, I would highly encourage the establishment at the beginning of the project of clear and shared guidelines for how success will be measured for the project. We may want to change the world, but we need to determine what parts get changed in 1, or 2, or 5, or 10 years and how these changes are measured.

It would also be wise to create, in the first year, a plan for the ultimate size and scope of the endeavor and for the turnover of parts of the project to the local school system. Any constructivist staff development effort should be working itself out of business from day 1. If we are there to empower the system staff, there should be a specific plan describing when and how we will leave and identifying who will do what after that. That is what staff and community development is all about.

At this writing, Bank Street is still working in the Newark Public Schools and still learning as much as teaching. Would we still do it again? Of course. In fact, we are already doing it again, in other cities and in other systems. As set out in our mission statement, we continue to "see in schools the opportunity to a better society." Working in and with urban public schools remains firmly rooted in our mission, history, and future.

16

Opening One's Heart to Love, Risk, and Change: One Staff Developer's Journey

Eileen Wasow

Eileen Wasow, who was an associate dean at Bank Street and also worked for New Beginnings before becoming executive director of the Ellington Fund, describes the unexpected difficulties she encountered adapting to the needs of Newark teachers. In her meditation on difference, Wasow explores her own upbringing under the tutelage of a grandmother's "fierce" love, progressive educational environments that encourage agency, choice, and self-determination, and new scientific research on the role of early nurturing. She exhorts educators to make respect a cornerstone of a shared language that would help us all to honor different ways of being in the world and to resist the impulse to judge others.

WHEN I LED MY FIRST WORKSHOP in Newark on a hot summer day in the middle of July, I remember packing my bag as if I were going to another country. I packed water, a snack, maps, train schedules, and some extra reading material. I took a New York City subway, a PATH train, and finally a car service to reach my destination. I remember the first workshop especially well because I was so pleased that after a slow start, a lively discussion ensued about involving parents in their children's education. But at the end of the workshop, after all my "good ideas" had been presented, the teachers began to express concern. I didn't really understand the Newark system. They would not even know who their students would be until the middle of September, when class rosters were finally settled.

As I reflect on that first workshop, I now realize the extent to which I had positioned myself as an "expert" from Bank Street. Little did I understand how I saw knowledge flow only from one side of the Hudson River to the other. I paid no attention to the understandings about family–school relations that the Newark teachers brought with them.

After 13 years of working in classrooms as an early childhood teacher, I certainly had firsthand experience of and respect for the knowledge that many teachers bring to the table. And, as an African-American teacher with experience in urban schools, I had expected to join easily with the Newark teachers to meet the challenges they faced. Yet the voice of authority that I had taken on as a staff developer obscured my capacity to listen to those teachers.

Only later, when I began to present workshops for New York City's Universal Pre-K program, did I begin to think more critically about my role as a staff developer. Only then, as I visited classrooms on a regular basis, and paid careful attention to what the teachers were saying, did I link listening with working collaboratively toward change. With each visit, I found myself opening to new risks and new areas of learning.

A year later, when I was asked to speak at the opening of the Bank Street–Newark Summer Institute, I had already begun to think long and hard about building a common language between teachers and staff developers, about valuing and protecting the cultures of these two diverse educational worlds, and finally about accepting the risks of opening one's heart to love and change. It is this last challenge that drives me to write this essay.

If staff developers are to find new ways to reach out to teachers, to relinquish their positions as experts, and to challenge conventional models of growth, then they must ask teachers to help them to create new maps of teaching and learning. The map I envision must honor the ground of those who have gone before. It must recognize the knowledge that teachers bring to defining their own professional development needs. Such a map must also designate past and current contested territories, border crossings, swamps, boundaries, and seemingly insurmountable barriers. Most important, the map must provide signs pointing to possibilities for collaboration.

At the start of this essay I described the physical journey that I took to Newark. But there was also a cultural-emotional dimension to the journey, one that I began to understand only when I returned home. Then I started to wonder how new developments in brain research might challenge our notions of teaching and learning. I also wondered about the impact of culture on how we as adults learn, which led me by extension to question our assumptions about how to teach children.

LINKING LEARNING, LOVE, AND CHANGE

Too often, we think of learning as solely the domain of the brain, a domain that we inherit from our parents as part of our genetic makeup. Recent research challenges the assumption that our capacity to learn is predetermined and fixed from conception. Neuroscientists have found that before birth, the brain is affected by conditions such as the nourishment, care, and stimulation that the individual receives. After birth, the developing brain is also affected by the quality of the interactions an infant has with the people and objects in its environment. The number and organization of neural pathways in the brain influence everything from the ability to recognize letters of the alphabet to the capacity to handle emotions (Ounce of Prevention Fund, 1996).

For those of us in early childhood education, this research confirms what we have always known about the importance of good early childhood care and teaching. But it also points to the integration of physical, emotional, and cognitive development in these early experiences.

Especially today, teachers strive to improve the academic achievement of young children. The foundation for success, however, begins in infancy. We know that babies thrive when they receive warm, responsive care. But most parents would be very surprised to learn that hugging, rocking, feeding, and singing to a baby not only meet the baby's basic needs but also directly affect the formation of the brain's neuropathways.

All the significant adults who come into contact with children in the crucial period from before birth through adolescence have a vital role to play. There is a direct correlation between children's early experiences and interactions that shape their emotional development and the wiring of their brains. If we want to help children achieve new standards and higher levels of academic achievement, then we must support the integration of their physical, cognitive, and emotional growth. We must recognize too how important it is to nurture children's total development with warm, responsive care.

Neuroscientists have amassed their data on the basis of years of research. I can only recount my understanding of these complex theories through the integration of my own observations and experiences over time. My stories paint a picture of the heart and brain as intertwined, and when the heart opens up, there is a powerful moment when learning rushes in.

I have a neighbor who lives down the street. Every year, she plants her impatiens in a mysterious order. She uses red, white, pink, and salmon-colored impatiens to spell out a message, and every year, the whole neighborhood waits to see what her new message will be. She works very quietly: She puts her impatiens plants in the ground a few at a time, and it is never quite clear when she is finished. But if you don't break the code quickly, the plants will grow too large and the message will disappear.

One evening, just about dusk, I was walking home from work and I thought to myself, she's finished the design. I stood on the sidewalk, next to this small patch of garden, and began to break the code. I was looking at the plants, reading the "letters" forward and backward, when suddenly I got it: "LOVE HEALS." I was so excited after reading this message that I wanted to go and hug my neighbor. The next morning on my way to work, I saw some young children—probably about 7 or 8 years old. They too were trying to decode the flowers' message. Of course, I was not going to reveal it, but I stood nearby and listened to them. I could hear them reading left to right, on the diagonal, top to bottom—trying to make sense of the encrypted message. Suddenly one child got it: "Love Heals," he shouted! At once they were all jumping up and down, like little contestants on *Jeopardy*. It was exciting to watch and I congratulated them on their discovery. The code-breaker turned to me and said: "I knew we were going to get it today. I just knew!"

My neighbor opens her heart to her community each year with a new gift—words set in flowers for us to puzzle over. In her own small way, she invites curiosity, affirms building meaning out of experience, rewards persistence, and—and without any fancy theories, she recognizes the link between heart and brain in the joy of learning.

The persistent struggle to make sense of something unfamiliar prompted by my neighbor reminds me how often my grandmother called me hardheaded when I was a very young child. I had no idea what she meant. I would ask her questions, and she would say, "Don't ask me so many questions. Don't be so hardheaded." In bed at night, I would feel my head. I would also feel my little sister's head, but her head did not feel any different from mine. My grandmother was a very strict, unsmiling person. I was afraid of her. I had no guidebook to help me decode what she was thinking about when she was so stern. Yet I cannot deny that she had high expectations for me and my siblings who were left in her care while my mother went to work each day.

Today, many educators still believe that we must prepare children of color for a harsh world and that warm, responsive care will not inure them to the inequities that they are bound to experience. But I am challenged to bridge the world of my grandmother's fierce love, which many of us as African Americans experienced when young, with the warm, responsive care endorsed by brain researchers. Having grown up with my grandmother's strict expectations and spending much of my adult life in progressive schools, I believe the only way to bridge the two worlds is to open our hearts—to acknowledge that high expectations and love can go hand in hand. By *love*, I do not mean an "anything goes, mushy" kind of love but the love like my grandmother had for me—a fierce love that starts with high expectations.

My worry is that, caught between the push for reform, testing, and standards, we will lose sight of the bigger picture. I know that teachers are under enormous pressure to set high expectations for their students. In an era when schools are being asked to do more, teachers are already staying late to help failing children and administrators are struggling to hold overburdened systems together. I realize that this may sound old-fashioned, but I argue that we can engage children to work at higher levels, whatever our teaching methodology and philosophy, if we love them with a fierceness from which they cannot walk away.

BUILDING A COMMON LANGUAGE: THE IMPACT OF CULTURE ON TEACHING AND LEARNING

To bridge the distances between Bank Street and Newark, we must build a common language, one that incorporates my grandmother's world of respect and discipline as well as worlds that embrace courage and compassion. On my own professional journeys, whether I am traveling to the South Bronx or to Newark, one of the key ingredients I have sought to pack is respect.

Recently, I asked the participants in a workshop to share stories with each other about how respect was taught in their families of origin. I joined in to round out the numbers so that everybody could work in pairs. Immediately I was plunged into a very lively discussion with my partner, who said that for her, respect had been embedded in everyday family routines. European-American in background, she stated emphatically that everyone just understood the importance of respect without referring to it directly. I shared a story with her about my grandmother and how respect was explicit, referred to in our daily exchanges and clearly understood by the oldest and youngest members of the family.

When asked how respect is taught in their current families, many parents and teachers concurred that things have changed. It just isn't so important anymore. Several parents of color, however, stated that respect continues to be a core value. They encourage their children to sit still in church, to behave courteously during family gatherings, and to honor their elders by being quiet, speaking only when spoken to.

I worry that children coming from backgrounds where "respect" is an overarching goal need a new map to guide them in a progressive classroom—a world of thinking, playing, taking risks, raising questions, "talking out" in ways that might be construed as "talking back" at home. Children who show initiative, creativity, coping skills, strengths, and mastery—these are the children that succeed in the ideal Bank Street classroom. The teacher who can tolerate this kind of questioning and agency on the part of children will likewise be deemed successful.

The question for me is, how do we get from my grandmother's world—my grandmother's code of respect—to this new world of progressive teaching and learning? I argue that as teachers, administrators, and staff developers, we need to take respect both ways in our journey from Newark to Bank Street and back again. By making respect a cornerstone of a shared language, staff developers and teachers can resist the rush to judge the child who is quiet or different, who doesn't rush over to materials like blocks, or who doesn't easily build verbal representations of her or his world.

The need for respect extends to children's families, who may be too easily labeled as without resources. All families have some resources and strengths. How do staff developers and teachers reach out and learn about them? How do staff developers support teachers, who, like certain children, value order, quiet, and respect for one's elders?

We can resist the rush to judge by opening our hearts to respecting and understanding difference. We need to listen more carefully to the child who has been rewarded for being quiet, observant, and slow to engage because it might be dangerous. Staff developers also need to respect the teacher who may be new to the Bank Street approach and skeptical about learning by doing. The very thing that we are asking of the children in our classrooms—the very task of making new meaning out of their experiences—we must ask of ourselves as well. We have much to learn from each other.

Another way to bridge the gulf that may exist between home and school is to review the literature on resiliency. Researchers (Werner & Smith, 1982) have observed that resilient children have the following characteristics in common:

- Problem-solving skills, such as the ability to plan, which enables a sense of control.
- A sense of purpose and belief in a bright future.
- Social skills such as flexibility, empathy, and caring.
- Strong communication skills, including a sense of humor.
- Autonomy, which includes developing one's sense of identity and power.

Emmy Werner (1990), a child psychologist, has studied resilient children in many different parts of the world. At a time when many other researchers are asking, "What puts children at risk for failure?" she asks a different question: "What are the factors that help children succeed?" Werner reminds us that there is a "shifting balance between stressful life events and events that heighten children's sense of vulnerability, and the protective factors in their lives which enhance their resiliency" (p. 111). This balance can change with each life-stage cycle and is sensitive to the culture and gender of the child. Werner continues:

> As long as the balance between stressful life events and protective factors is manageable, then children can cope. When the stressful life events outweigh protective factors, even the most resilient child can develop problems. (p. 111)

In our roles as caring adults, it is critical that we strive to restore this balance either by decreasing the child's exposure to intense and chronic life stresses or by increasing the number of protective factors. As my neighbor who loves to garden might say, we need to increase the number of opportunities where the child can experience firsthand that "Love Heals."

I know that it is often a racist world into which we send our children. Some educators may say, forget this progressive education stuff, this community-of-learners talk. Teach children what they need to succeed in the world. Some educators of color may think that by being stern, we can help toughen up our children, so they never have to get in touch with the pain of discrimination based on race, sexual orientation, class, gender, or special needs. Teachers of color who were raised with stern codes of behavior that rewarded passive learning need more opportunities to examine the contradictions between their own experience and new expectations for children that involve active problem-solving and critical thinking.

As we weigh the potentials for vulnerability and resilience in children, so must we weigh the benefits of opening our hearts to change.

One benefit is that current practice will be challenged. Teachers must confront the images and educational rhetoric that portray children in urban schools as "at risk." As collaborators from both sides of the river, we have the chance to coconstruct a new curriculum, building on the life experiences and resilience that children bring to school. We can model the process of learning from one another much as we would like the children to learn from each other and from us.

Another benefit is that we will learn new things about progressive education. How does it work in a large urban setting? How will New Beginnings take shape over the next years as the teachers, families, and even the children of Newark come to own it? What will be the result of their ongoing engagement with this intentionally democratic approach to education?

Yet another benefit is the inevitable reflection that comes with change. Reflection can be brutal, but it can also be refreshing and energizing. Learning in the midst of a rapidly evolving and constantly challenging situation requires practitioners to be self-aware and, in turn, to be conscious of their impact on others (Schon, 1987). This vision of self-awareness—self in the change process, in a group, in a community of learners—is what gives me hope for the collaboration between Bank Street and the Newark Public Schools.

My grandmother hovers near me still. I carry her voice around with me, though, more often now, I am willing to hear its love rather than its sternness. I think I understand better why she was so strict. I just wish she might have leavened her sternness sometimes with a hug and praise for a job well done. This is the challenge for us to carry on. This is the map we must color in, giving shape to the borders and boundaries as meaning emerges out of our shared experiences.

Appendix

Student Outcomes on District and State Assessments for the 1996–1997 New Beginnings Kindergarten Cohort

Rosemarie Kopacsi

ANK STREET COLLEGE RESEARCHERS have completed three qualitative studies of the Newark New Beginnings collaboration between Bank Street College and the Newark Public Schools, which highlighted the process as well as implementation strengths and challenges over the years (Schwartz & Silin, 1998; Schwartz, Silin, & Miserendino, 1999; Silin & Schwartz, 2000). These studies elaborate upon the contexts within which change occurred and identify shifts in program focus over the years. These reports also delineate the roles played by the Newark Public Schools and Bank Street College as partners in building capacity to support the district's whole school reform process.

The Office of Planning, Evaluation and Testing of the Newark Public Schools completed several reports on student outcomes, which focused on tracking the progress of the first New Beginnings student cohort. After the first (1996–1997) school year, Bank Street College expanded its New Beginnings interventions to include additional grade levels (1 to 3) at some district schools. Four years of test-score analyses and comparative findings are summarized in the four tables included in this appendix. The tables show comparisons of test outcomes for the first New Beginnings cohort at the end of kindergarten, second grade, third grade, and fourth grade with outcomes for cohorts of students that did not receive New Beginnings interventions. Test scores were disaggregated by the number of years of New Beginnings classroom supports that students in the first cohort received.

Table A.1. A Comparison of Kindergarten Outcomes on District Kindergarten Test*

1997 District Criterion-Referenced Test	New Beginnings (*n* = 289) Avg. % Correct	Control Group (*n* = 930) Avg. % Correct
Reading	89.2* (9.8) SD**	83.1 (14.2) SD
Math	88.1* (10.6) SD	81.8 (17.5) SD

*Significant at .01.
**SD stands for standard deviation.

- Comparisons of outcomes for the first New Beginnings cohort with the comparison cohort presented in Table A.1 show that significantly higher percentages of New Beginnings students passed the district criterion-referenced kindergarten tests in reading and math.
- Comparisons presented in Table A.2, show significantly higher outcomes on the second-grade Stanford 9 norm-referenced test in reading and math for the New Beginnings cohort. In particular, findings show that students in New Beginnings classes who received continuous program supports for 3 years benefited the most when test scores were compared with those of students who received less intensive and/or interrupted services, or no program interventions at all. These differences were statistically significant in reading and math in total and subtest skill areas.
- Comparisons presented in Table A.3 show third-grade test outcomes on the Stanford 9. These findings show that, although students who received 3 and 4 years of New Beginnings program

Table A.2. A Comparison of Second-Grade Stanford 9 Outcomes Disaggregated by Number of Years of New Beginnings Support*

1999 Stanford 9	Kindergarten Yr Only NB (*n* = 35)	Any 2 Years of NB Supports (*n* = 66)	3 Years of NB Supports (*n* = 73)	Control Cohort (*n* = 460)
Reading	45.5 NCES** (19.5) SD	39.4 NCES (15.7) SD	55.8* NCES (17.8) SD	44.0 NCES (21.7) SD
Math	45.7 NCES (18.3) SD	44.9 NCES (22.7) SD	59.2* NCES (22.8) SD	46.8 NCES (24.2) SD

*Significant at .01.
**NCES stands for normal curve equivalent scores.

Table A.3. A Comparison of Third-Grade Stanford 9 Outcomes Disaggregated by Number of Years of New Beginnings Support*

2000 Stanford 9	Kindergarten Yr Only NB (n = 33)	Any 2 Years of NB Supports (n = 67)	Any 3 & 4 Years of NB Supports (n = 74)	Control Cohort (n = 212)
Reading	42.8 NCES (20.0) SD	35.9 NCES (16.9) SD	46.5* NCES (20.3) SD	38.5 NCES (20.4) SD
Math	52.0 NCES (23.1) SD	38.4* NCES (19.6) SD	50.9 NCES (24.9) SD	45.7 NCES (23.9) SD

*Significant at .01.

supports showed significantly higher outcomes in reading and somewhat higher outcomes in math, students who received 2 years of New Beginnings classroom interventions demonstrated the weakest outcomes among all cohorts in both reading and math. Cohort differences in academic outcomes are likely influenced by multiple factors, including a complex district-wide whole school reform transitioning at all schools, particularly during the 1997–1998 and 1998–1999 time period.

• Comparisons presented in Table A.4 show student outcomes on the New Jersey State Assessment mandated at the end of fourth grade. The percentage of students who achieved proficiency on the State Elementary School Proficiency Assessment (ESPA) in the combined 3- and 4-year New Beginnings cohort was some-

Table A.4. A Comparison of Fourth-Grade ESPA Outcomes Disaggregated by Number of Years of New Beginnings Support*

2001 ESPA NJ State Assessment	Kindergarten Yr Only NB (n = 28) % Proficient	Any 2 Years of NB Supports (n = 42) % Proficient	Any 3 & 4 Years of NB Supports (n = 67) % Proficient	Non-NB Schools Comparison Cohort (n = 2197) % Proficient
Language Arts Literacy	53.6	42.5	56.3	52.2
Mathematics	35.7	19.0	37.3	32.7
Science	57.1	50.0	61.9	56.7

*Comparisons of proportion differences were not statistically significant

what higher than the percentage of students who achieved proficiency in the comparison cohort. These differences, however, were not statistically significant. Again, the 2-year New Beginnings cohort, which included many of the students from the prior year's 2-year New Beginnings cohort, continued to show the weakest outcomes at fourth grade.

NOTES

a) The interpretation of findings presented in Tables A.1–A.4 is limited by a number of factors. Academic outcomes may be confounded by influences simultaneously impacting student learning, including varied district- and school-level educational initiatives and support services. In addition, behavioral outcomes related to New Beginnings that impact on student learning, motivation, inquiry, and social skills cannot be captured by the very limited analysis of test data. Other contributing factors over the 5-year tracking period include school-level differences related to whole school reform model selection and implementation, as well as the cohort attrition rates of the research studies.

b) All of the 4 years of test score analyses included here show comparisons of student outcomes for students who attended New Beginnings classes with those of students who did not participate in New Beginnings classes. Student outcomes in Tables A.2, A.3, and A.4 were disaggregated by the number of years of New Beginnings classroom supports that students received. (Multiple years of supports were not necessarily consecutive.) The students who received 3 and 4 years of New Beginnings supports were combined (as one) to improve the representative nature of the cohort.

c) Student mobility as well as the absence of a central data management system for tracking student data longitudinally made matching of students with test scores difficult. The matching of individual students with test scores was sometimes interrupted from year to year. A better than 50% test score matching rate was achieved overall with the original cohort database.

d) *ANOVA* procedures were used for the comparison of normal curve equivalent scores on the second- and third-grade reading and math Stanford 9 tests. The post hoc statistics provided multiple comparisons of means tests to identify the significance of differences between cohorts. Levene's Test of Variances was used to control for differences in variance. At fourth grade, a z test of independent sample proportions provided a measure of the significance of differences for the New Beginnings cohorts with a nonparticipating comparison cohort.

References

Antler, J. (1987). *Lucy Sprague Mitchell: The making of a modern woman.* New Haven, CT: Yale University Press.

Anyon, J. (1994). Teacher development and reform in an inner-city school. *Teachers College Record, 96*(1), 14–31.

Anyon, J. (1997). *Ghetto schooling: A political economy of urban educational reform.* New York: Teachers College Press.

Apple, M. (1990). *Ideology and curriculum.* New York: Routledge.

Aronowitz, S., & Giroux, H. (1991). *Postmodern education.* Minneapolis: University of Minnesota Press.

Association for Children of New Jersey. (2000). *Kids count New Jersey 2000: State and county profiles of child well-being.* Newark: Author.

Biber, B. (1984). *Early education and psychological development.* New Haven, CT: Yale University Press.

Blizzard, G. S. (1990). *Come look with me: Enjoying art with children.* Charlottesville, VA: Thomasson-Grant.

Blizzard, G. S. (1992). *Come look with me: Exploring landscape art with children.* Palm Beach, FL: Lickle Publishing.

Bredekamp, S., & Copple, C. (Eds.). (1997). *Developmentally appropriate practice in early childhood programs.* Washington, DC: National Association for the Education of Young Children.

Clarke, W., & Wasley, P. (1999). Renewing schools and smarter kids: Promises for democracy. *Phi Delta Kappan,* 590–596.

Cochran-Smith, M. (1995). Color blindness and basket making are not the answers: Confronting the dilemmas of race, culture, and language diversity in teacher education. *American Educational Research Journal, 32*(3), 493–522.

Cohen, D. (1972). *The learning child.* New York: Schocken Books.

Comer, J. P., & Poussaint, A. F., M.D. (1992). *Raising African-American children.* New York: Penguin Books USA. (Original work published in 1975)

Community Training and Assistance Center. (2000). *Myths and realities: The impact of the state takeover on students and school in Newark.* Boston: Author. (Available from CTAC, 30 Winter Street, Boston, MA 02108)

Cremin, L. (1961). *The transformation of the school: Progressivism in American education 1876–1957.* New York: Vintage Books.

Cuffaro, H. (1995). *Experimenting with the world: John Dewey and the early childhood classroom.* New York: Teachers College Press.

Cuffaro, H. (2000). *Educational standards in a democracy: Questioning process and consequences.* Child Development Institute, Sarah Lawrence College, Occasional Paper # 4.

Cuffaro, H. K., Nager, N., & Shapiro, E. K. (2000). The developmental-interaction approach at Bank Street College. In J. L. Roopnarine & J. E. Johnson (Eds.), *Approaches to early childhood education* (3rd ed.). Englewood Cliffs, NJ: Prentice Hall.

Datnow, A., & Castellano, M. (2000). Teachers' responses to success for all: How beliefs, experiences, and adaptations shape implementation. *American Educational Research Journal, 37*(3), 775–800.

Delpit, L. (1986). Skills and other dilemmas of a progressive Black educator. *Harvard Educational Review, 56*(4), 379–385.

Delpit, L. (1988). The silenced dialogue: Power and pedagogy in educating other people's children. *Harvard Educational Review, 58*(3), 280–298.

Delpit, L. (1995). *Other people's children: Cultural conflict in the classroom.* New York: The New Press.

Desimore, L. (2000). *Making comprehensive school reform work.* Urban Diversity Series No. 112. ERIC Clearinghouse on Urban Education and the Institute for Urban and Minority Education. New York: Teachers College, Columbia University.

Dewey, J. (1956). *The school and society: The child and the curriculum.* Chicago: University of Chicago Press. (Original work published 1900)

Dewey, J. (1966). *Democracy and education.* New York: Free Press. (Original work published 1916)

Dewey, J. (1972). *Experience and education.* New York: Collier Books. (Original work published 1938)

DuBois, W. E. B. (1993). *The souls of Black folk.* New York: Dover. (Original work published 1903)

Education Commission of the States. (1999). *Comprehensive school reform: Five lessons from the field.* (Available from ECS, 7077 17th Street, Suite 2700, Denver, CO 80202-3427)

Education Resources Group. (1996). *Vision 21: Three year summary of evaluation findings, 1994–1996.* (Available from Education Resources Group, 220 Nassau Street, Suite 250A, Princeton, NJ 08542)

Ellsworth, J., & Ames, L. J. (1998). *Critical perspectives on project Head Start: Revisioning the hope and the challenge.* Albany: State University of New York Press.

Elmore, R. (1995). Structural reform and educational practice. *Educational Researcher, 24*(9), 23–26.

Erlichson, B., & Goertz, M. (2001). *Implementing whole school reform in New Jersey: Year two.* (Available from the Department of Public Policy and Center for Government Services, Edward J. Bloustein School of Planning and Public Policy, Rutgers, The State University of New Jersey, 33 Livingston Avenue, Suite 200, New Brunswick, NJ 08901-1979)

Erlichson, B., Goertz, M., & Turnbull, B. (1999). *Implementing whole school reform in New Jersey: Year one in the first cohort schools*. (Available from the Department of Public Policy and Center for Government Services, Edward J. Bloustein School of Planning and Public Policy, Rutgers, The State University of New Jersey, 33 Livingston Avenue, Suite 200, New Brunswick, NJ 08901-1979)

Feldman, R., Horton, D., & Niemeyer, J. H. (1975). *School intervention project. Report to the Edna McConnell Clark Foundation*. New York: Bank Street College.

Fine, M., Weis, L., Powell, L. C., & Wong, L. M. (Eds.). (1997). *Off White: Readings on race, power, and society*. New York: Routledge.

Fink, D., & Stoll, L. (1998). Educational change: Easier said than done. In A. Hargreaves, A. Lieberman, M. Fullan, & D. Hopkins (Eds.), *International handbook of educational change* (pp. 297–321). Boston: Kluwer Academic.

Fordham, S. (1996). *Blacked out: Dilemmas of race, identity, and success at Capital High*. Chicago: University of Chicago Press.

Freire, P. (1986). *Pedagogy of the oppressed* (M. B. Ramos, Trans.). New York: Seabury Press.

Fullan, M. (1982). *The meaning of educational change*. New York: Teachers College Press.

Fullan, M. (1991). *The new meaning of educational change*. New York: Teachers College Press.

Fullan, M. (1998). The meaning of educational change: A quarter of a century of learning. In A. Hargreaves A. Liebermann, M. Fullan, & D. Hopkins (Eds.), *International handbook of educational change* (pp. 214–228). Boston: Kluwer Academic.

Fullan, M. (1999). *Change forces: The sequel*. Philadelphia: The Falmer Press.

Gilkeson, E. C., Bowman, G. W., Smithberg, L. M., & Rhine, W. R. (1981). Bank Street model: A developmental–interaction approach. In W. R. Rhine (Ed.), *Making schools more effective: New directions from Follow Through*. (pp. 249–288). New York: Academic Press.

Greene, M. (1995). *Releasing the imagination*. San Francisco: Jossey-Bass.

Greenfield, P. M. (1994). Independence and interdependence as developmental scripts: Implications for theory, research, and practice. In P. M. Greenfield & R. R. Cocking (Eds.), *Cross-cultural roots of minority child development* (pp. 1–37). Hillsdale, NJ: Lawrence Erlbaum Associates.

Hale, J. E. (1982). *African-American children, their roots, culture and learning styles*. Provo, UT: Brigham Young University Press.

Hargreaves, A. (1998). Pushing the boundaries of educational change. In A. Hargreaves, A. Lieberman, M. Fullan, & D. Hopkins (Eds.), *International handbook of educational change* (pp. 281–294). Boston: Kluwer Academic.

Hecht, M. L., Collier, M. J., & Ribeau, S. A. (1993). *African American communication: Ethnic identity and cultural interpretation*. Newbury Park, CA: Sage.

Henrich, C. C., Brown, J. L., & Aber, J. L. (1999). Evaluating the effectiveness of school-based violence prevention: Developmental approaches. *Social Policy Report, Society for Research in Child Development, 13*(3).

House, E., Glass, G. V., McLean, L. D., & Walker, D. F. (1978). No simple answer: Critique of the Follow Through evaluation. *Harvard Educational
Review, 48*, 128–160.

Hoyle, E. (1989). The primary school teacher as professional. In M. Galton &
A. Blyth (Eds.), *Handbook of primary education in Europe* (pp. 415–432).
London: David Fulton.

Jacobs, A. (2002, May 10). Newark's competing visions of itself. *The New York
Times*, p. A30.

Johnston, R. (2000, May 31). N.J. takeover of Newark found to yield gains, but
lack clear goals. *Education Week*.

Kalyanpur, M., & Harry, B. (1999). *Culture in special education: Building reciprocal family–professional relationships*. Baltimore: Paul H. Brookes.

Kohl, H. (1967). *36 children*. New York: The New American Library.

Kopacsi, R., & Hochwald, E. (1997). *Evaluation of New Beginnings kindergarten model first year: 1996–1997*. Office of Planning, Evaluation, & Testing, Newark Public Schools. (Available from Project New Beginnings, Bank
Street College of Education, 610 West 112th Street, New York, NY 10025)

Kopacsi, R., & Onsongo, E. (1999). *New Beginnings student outcomes revisited
in 1999: Cohort comparisons on student achievement and attendance*.
Office of Planning, Evaluation, & Testing, Newark Public Schools. (Available from The Newark Public Schools, 2 Cedar Street, Newark, NJ 07102)

Kozol, J. (1992). *Savage inequalities: Children in America's schools*. New York:
Harperperennial Library.

Ladson-Billings, Gloria. (1994). *The dreamkeepers: Successful teachers of African American children*. San Francisco: Jossey-Bass.

Ladson-Billings, G. (1995). Toward a theory of culturally relevant pedagogy.
American Educational Research Journal, 35, 465–491.

Lesch, J. (2000). *Insider/outsider relationships: Reconsidering outside staff
development through the prism of race, class, and culture*. Paper presented
at the annual meeting of the American Educational Research Association,
New Orleans, LA.

Levin, H. M. (1998). Educational performance standards and the economy.
Educational Researcher, 27(4), 4–10.

Linn, R. L. (2000). Assessments and accountability. *Educational Researcher,
29*(2), 4–16.

Little, J. (1993). *Teachers' professional development in a climate of educational
reform*. National Center for Restructuring Education, Schools, and Teaching. New York: Teachers College, Columbia University.

Lynch, E. W., & Hanson, M. J. (Eds.). (1998). *Developing cross-cultural competence: A guide for working with children and families* (2nd ed.). Baltimore: Paul H. Brookes.

McIntosh, P. (1989). White privilege: Unpacking the invisible knapsack. *Peace
and Freedom, 49*(4), 10–12.

McLaughlin, M. (1976). Implementation as mutual adaptation: Change in classroom organization. *Teachers College Record, 77*(3), 339–351.

McLaughlin, M. (1998). Listening and learning from the field: Tales of policy implementation and situated practice. In A. Hargreaves, A. Lieberman, M. Fullan, & D. Hopkins (Eds.), *International handbook of educational change* (pp. 70–84). Boston: Kluwer Academic.

McNaughton, G. (2000). *Rethinking gender in early childhood education.* Sydney, Australia: Allen & Unwin.

Meier, D. (1995). *The power of their ideas.* Boston: Beacon Press.

Meier, D. (2000). *Will standards save the public schools?* Boston: Beacon Press.

Meier, T. (1999). The case for ebonics as part of exemplary teacher preparation. In C. T. Adger, D. Christian, & O. Taylor (Eds.), *Making the connection: Language and academic achievement among African American students* (pp. 97–114). McHenry, IL: Center for Applied Linguistics and Delta Systems Co.

Micklethwait, L. (1993). *Child's book of art: Great paintings, first words.* London: DK Publishing.

Mitchell, A., & David, J. (1992). *Explorations with young children: A curriculum guide.* Beltsville, MD: Gryphon House.

Mitchell, L. S. (1950). *Our children and our schools.* New York: Simon and Schuster.

Mitchell, L. S. (1991). *Young geographers.* New York: Bank Street College of Education. (Original work published in New York by John Day, 1934)

Mitchell, L. S. (2000). Social studies for future teachers. In N. Nager & E. K. Shapiro, *Revisiting a progressive pedagogy: The developmental-interaction approach* (pp. 125–137). Albany: State University of New York Press.

Nager, N., & Shapiro, E. K. (2000). *Revisiting a progressive pedagogy: The developmental-interaction approach.* Albany: State University of New York Press.

New, R. S. (1994). Culture, child development, and developmentally appropriate practice: Teachers as collaborative researchers. In B. L. Mallory & R. S. New (Eds.), *Diversity and developmentally appropriate practices: Challenges for early childhood education* (pp. 65–83). New York: Teachers College Press.

New Jersey Department of Education. (1993, April). *Comprehensive compliance investigation of the Newark school district: Vol. I. Executive summary.*

Noddings, N. (1984). *Caring: A feminine approach to ethics and moral education.* Berkeley: University of California Press.

Oakes, J., & Lipton, M. (1999). *Teaching to change the world.* New York: McGraw-Hill.

Ogbu, J. U. (1999). Beyond language: Ebonics, proper English, and identity in a Black-American speech community. *American Educational Research Journal, 36*(2), 147–182.

Ounce of Prevention Fund. (1996). *Starting smart: How early experiences affect the brain.* (Available from Ounce of Prevention Fund, 122 South Michigan Avenue, Suite 2050, Chicago, IL 60603)

Paley, V. (1992). *You can't say you can't play.* Cambridge, MA: Harvard University Press.

Parham, T. A., White, J. L., & Ajamu, A. (1999). *The psychology of Blacks: An African centered perspective* (3rd ed.). Upper Saddle River, NJ: Prentice-Hall.

Phillips, C. B. (1994). The movement of African American children through sociocultural contexts: A case of conflict resolution. In B. L. Mallory & R. S. New (Eds.), *Diversity and developmentally appropriate practices: Challenges for early childhood education* (pp. 137–154). New York: Teachers College Press.

Pizzo, P. D. (1993). Parent empowerment and childcare regulation. *Young Children, 48*(6), 9–12.

Project New Beginnings. (2000). *New Beginnings.* (Available from Project New Beginnings, Bank Street College of Education, 610 West 112th Street, New York, NY 10025)

Putnam, R., & Borko, H. (2000). What do new views of knowledge and thinking have to say about research on teacher learning? *Educational Researcher, 29*(1), 4–15.

Ravitch, D. (2000). *Left back: A century of failed school reform.* New York: Simon and Schuster.

Reid, K. (2001, February 14). Newark sues state, district over losses. *Education Week.*

Richardson, V. (1992). The agenda-setting dilemma in a constructivist staff development process. *Teaching & Teacher Education, 8,* 287–300.

Scheurich, J. J. (1993). Toward a White discourse on White racism. *Educational Researcher, 22*(8), 5–10.

Schon, D. (1987). *Educating the reflective practitioner.* Paper presented at the American Educational Research Association, Washington, DC.

School Reform News. (1999, May). Takeovers don't bring turnaround in student achievement [On-line]. Available: http://www.heartland.org/education/may99/turn.htm

Schwartz, F., & Silin, J. (1998). *Project New Beginnings, the second year.* (Available from Project New Beginnings, Bank Street College of Education, 610 West 112th Street, New York, NY 10025.)

Schwartz, F., & Silin, J. (2002). Alysha's day: Progressive education as school reform. Manuscript submitted for publication.

Schwartz, F., Silin, J., & Miserendino, J. (1999). *Project New Beginnings, the third year.* (Available from Project New Beginnings, Bank Street College of Education, 610 West 112th Street, New York NY 10025)

Shapiro, E., & Biber, B. (1972). The education of young children: A developmental-interaction point of view. *Teachers College Record, 74*(1), 55–79.

Shapiro, E. K., & Nager, N. (1999). *The developmental-interaction approach to education: Retrospect and prospect.* (Occasional Paper Series). New York: Bank Street College of Education.

Silin, J., & Schwartz, F. (2000). *Project New Beginnings, the fourth year.* (Available from Project New Beginnings, Bank Street College of Education, 610 West 112th Street, New York, NY 10025.)

Slee, R., Weiner, G., & Tomlinson, S. (1998). *School effectiveness for whom?* London: Falmer Press.

Thompson, A. (1998). Not the color purple: Black feminist lessons for educational caring. *Harvard Educational Review, 68*(4), 522–554.

Tyack, D., & Cuban, L. (1995). *Tinkering toward utopia: A century of public school reform.* Cambridge: Harvard University Press.

Werner, E. (1990). Protective factors and individual resilience. In S. Meisels & J. Shonkoff (Eds.), *Handbook of early intervention* (pp. 101–104). New York: Press Syndicate of the University of Cambridge.

Werner, E., & Smith, R. (1982). *Vulnerable but invincible: A longitudinal study of resilient children and youth.* New York: McGraw-Hill.

Williams, L. R. (1999). Determining the early childhood curriculum: The evolution of goals and strategies through consonance and controversy. In C. Seefeldt (Ed.), *The early childhood curriculum: Current findings in theory and practice* (3rd ed., pp. 1–26). New York: Teachers College Press.

Winsor, C. B. (Ed.). (1973). *Experimental schools revisited: Bulletins of the Bureau of Educational Experiments.* New York: Agathon Press.

Yenawine, P. (1991a). *Colors.* New York: Museum of Modern Art, Delacorte Press.

Yenawine, P. (1991b). *Lines.* New York: Museum of Modern Art, Delacorte Press.

Yenawine, P. (1991c). *Shapes.* New York: Museum of Modern Art, Delacorte Press.

Yenawine, P. (1991d). *Stories.* New York: Museum of Modern Art, Delacorte Press.

Ziebarth, T. (2001). *Policy brief: Accountability—Rewards/sanctions—State takeovers and reconstitutions.* Colorado: Education Commission of the States. (Available from ECS, 7077 17th Street, Suite 2700, Denver, CO 80202-3427)

Zigler, E. F. (1981). Forward. In W. R. Rhine (Ed.), *Making schools more effective: New directions from Follow Through* (pp. xiii–xcii). New York: Academic Press.

Zimiles, H., & Mayer, R. (with Wickens, E). (1980). *Bringing child-centered education to the public schools: A study of school intervention.* New York: Bank Street College of Education.

About the Editors and Contributors

Nancy Balaban, is a member of the faculty of the Bank Street Graduate School of Education. She is the author of *Starting School: From Separation to Independence: A Guide for Early Childhood Teachers* and the author responsible for the revision of *Observing and Recording the Behavior of Young Children*.

Marva Wright Banks, wife of Judge Banks, is one of 12 children born to Mary and William Kettles and is a lifelong resident of Newark, N.J. She has seven children, eight grandchildren, and two great-grandchildren, and has been an employee of the Newark Public Schools for the past 30 years.

Betsy Blachly came to Bank Street College in 1970 as a student in the guitar workshop. After that she was a music teacher at the New Lincoln School and a percussion and timpani student at Mannes College of Music. In 1976 she became the music specialist in the Bank Street School for Children's Lower School and Family Center. She is an adjunct instructor in the Bank Street Graduate School and spent two fruitful years as a consultant for Project New Beginnings. She plans to complete her master's degree in music therapy at New York University by June 2003.

Joan Bojsza has been teaching for 27 years. She has also worked with children as a volunteer with Girl Scouts, PTA, church youth work, and library summer reading programs. Joan has been teaching in Newark for 11 years and has been with the New Beginnings project since its inception. She is married to Walter Bojsza and they have two daughters, Elizabeth (24) and Katherine (21).

Born and raised in Newark, N.J., **Marion Bolden** is the current superintendent of the Newark Public Schools. She is a graduate of Montclair State University with a B.A. in math education and an M.A. in teaching. She is a member of Sigma Gamma Sorority. Ms. Bolden began her career as a math teacher at Barringer High School in Newark during the 1960s. She was the director of the Office of Mathematics from 1989 to 1996 and associate superintendent of teaching and learning from 1996 to 1999. During that period she also served as interim assistant superintendent of School Leadership Team II. Ms. Bolden is the proud mother of two daughters.

Lillian Burke is the principal of Clinton Avenue Elementary School, one of the first schools to implement the New Beginnings program. She has been an educator in New Jersey for 31 years, having worked as an elementary classroom teacher, an ESL teacher, a curriculum specialist, an adjunct professor at both Kean College and Union County College, and the vice-principal of Bragaw Elementary. Ms. Burke is a member of the board of trustees of the Principal's Center for the Garden State.

Ethel Marie Cotten has lived in Newark, N.J., for more than 15 years. She has worked for the Newark Public Schools for 25 years in early childhood classes. She values the enthusiasm the children bring to learning and her involvement in Project New Beginnings.

Evangeline Dent was born in North Carolina. She graduated from Battin High School in Elizabeth, N.J. Ms. Dent is the mother of four children and grandmother of two. She has worked for the Newark Public Schools for 29 years.

A graduate of Montclair State University, **Lenore Furman** has taught kindergarten for 20 years. She is one of the original 16 New Beginnings teachers, and educators throughout the district visit her model classroom. She also teaches courses for those interested in learning more about the New Beginnings approach.

Before becoming superintendent of the Atlanta Public Schools in July 1999, **Beverly L. Hall**, was state district superintendent of the Newark Public Schools. Prior to that she served as deputy chancellor for instruction of the New York City Public Schools, superintendent of Community School District 27 in Queens, N.Y., and principal of Jun-

ior High School 113 and Public School 282 in Brooklyn, N.Y. Dr. Hall
and her husband Luis have one son, Jason, who is a graduate of St. Johns
University.

As teacher, school leader, and consultant, **Margot Hammond** has worked
with children and families in a variety of capacities for more than 25
years. She is a strong advocate for quality childcare and education for
children and families, and is deeply committed to professional preparation for their teachers and caregivers. Former director of the Family
Center at Bank Street College, Ms. Hammond currently works as program coordinator and staff developer for Project New Beginnings. She
is a frequent presenter at early childhood conferences and the author of
Let's Get Cooking, a guide to cooking with young children written for
parents and teachers.

Kathleen Hayes taught 4- and 5-year-olds in the Bank Street School for
Children for 10 years before becoming a staff developer for Project New
Beginnings. She is also the author of *Classroom Routines That Really
Work for Pre-K and K* (Scholastic, 2001) and a contributing writer to
McGraw-Hill's Pre-K Math Series, 2002, and their Pre-K Reading and
Social Studies Series, 2003.

Sandra Heintz has been working with young children in various capacities for most of her life, starting as a summer camp counselor in the
early 1970s and later serving as a camp director, a day-care director, an
education supervisor for a Head Start agency, and, most important, a
teacher. In her current position as resource teacher coordinator for the
Newark Public Schools, she continues to enjoy making music with
children and teachers in workshops and classrooms and with her own
two marvelously musical teenagers.

Augusta Souza Kappner is the president of Bank Street College of Education. Prior to assuming the presidency, she served as an assistant
secretary in the United States Department of Education during the
Clinton administration. She has also served as the president of the Bor-
ough of Manhattan Community College and acting president of City
College, both parts of the City University of New York.

Rosemarie Kopacsi, is the research supervisor, Office of Planning, Evaluation and Testing, Newark Public Schools, where she manages and su-
pervises educational research projects and collaborates with community

partners and program administrators on the role of evaluation in program planning and development. Dr. Kopacsi is the author of two recent publications: R. Kopacsi and E. Walker, "Multiple Voices and Mixed Methodologies to Support Comprehensive School Reform," a paper presented at the annual meeting of the American Educational Research Association, New Orleans, LA, April 24–28, 2000; and R. Kopacsi and E. Hochwald, "Evaluation of a Child-centered Kindergarten Model in Newark Public Schools: 1996–1997," in *ERS Spectrum: Journal of School Research and Information, 16*(4), Fall 1998, pp. 32–39.

Lesley Koplow, is the director of Creating Emotionally Responsive Pre-K for Children, a collaborative project between Bank Street College and the New York City Department of Education, and coordinator of mental health for Project New Beginnings. She is also a psychotherapist in private practice and the author of books on child mental health.

Gloria Ladson-Billings is a professor in the department of curriculum and instruction at the University of Wisconsin-Madison and a former Senior Fellow in Urban Education at the Annenberg Institute for School Reform at Brown University. Her research interests concern the relationship between culture and schooling, particularly successful teaching and learning for African-American students. Her publications include *The Dreamkeepers: Successful Teachers of African American Children, The Dictionary of Multicultural Education* (with Carl A. Grant), *Crossing Over to Canaan: The Journey of New Teachers in Diverse Classrooms* (May 2001), and numerous journal articles and book chapters. Ladson-Billings has won many awards for her scholarship, including the 1989–1990 National Academy of Education Spencer Post Doctoral Fellowship, the Early Career Contribution Award (1995) of the Committee on the Role and Status of Minorities in the American Educational Research Association, the Multicultural Research Award (1995) from the National Association of Multicultural Education, the Palmer O. Johnson Award (1996) for an outstanding article appearing in an AERA-sponsored publication, the Mary Ann Raywid Award (1997) from the Society of Professors of Education, and the H. I. Romnes Award (1998) for outstanding research potential from the University of Wisconsin-Madison.

After starting her career as a dancer, **Judith W. Lesch** taught dance at Teachers College while completing her doctorate there. She worked as a classroom special education teacher in public preschools and elementary grades for 15 years. She is currently an advisor/instructor at Bank Street College of Education.

Carol Lippman has been the director of Project New Beginnings since its inception in 1996. Prior to that, she was the director of Project Healthy Choices and a member of the graduate faculty at Bank Street College. She is the author of "Developmental Reality: Helping Teachers Deal With Violence in Children's Lives," in *Revisiting a Progressive Pedagogy: The Developmental-Interaction Approach*, edited by N. Nager & E. Shapiro. She has two master's degrees in early childhood education, a doctorate in social work, and is currently a candidate at the New York University Postdoctoral Program in Psychotherapy and Psychoanalysis.

Catherine M. McFarland is the executive director of the Victoria Foundation. Civic contributions and board affiliations include NJPAC Council of Trustees, Community Foodbank of New Jersey, Newark Advocates for Children, Local Initiatives Support Corporation, founding member of Newark Emergency Services for Families, and vestryman at Trinity Wall Street. Ms. McFarland graduated with highest honors from Rutgers University and was later awarded an honorary Doctor of Laws from Bloomfield College.

Mary Reaves has worked in the Newark Public Schools for 30 years. She is the mother of three grown children and has six grandchildren. Ms. Reaves earned a B.S. in public policy at St. Peter's College and a degree in early childhood education from Kean University in Union, N.J.

Edna K. Shapiro, research psychologist emeritus, is a developmental psychologist whose research at Bank Street College has focused on the integration of developmental and educational concepts, and evaluation of educational programs. Recently, with Nancy Nager, she coedited *Revisiting a Progressive Pedagogy: The Developmental-Interaction Approach* (State University of New York, 2000).

Jonathan G. Silin is co-director of research for Project New Beginnings and a member of the graduate faculty, Bank Street College of Education. He is the author of *Sex, Death, and the Education of Children: Our Passion for Ignorance in the Age of AIDS* (Teachers College Press, 1995) and coproducer of *Children Talk About AIDS* (Teachers College Press, 1999). Before receiving his doctorate in curriculum and teaching from Teachers College, Columbia University, he was a classroom teacher and taught in a variety of early childhood settings.

Felice Wagman taught kindergarten through third grade at various times during her 12-year career in the Newark Public Schools. Currently, she works as a mental health consultant for Project New Beginnings. She is a proud mother of 2½-year-old Sarah.

Eileen Wasow is currently the executive director of the Ellington Fund, the nonprofit fundraising arm of the Duke Ellington School of the Arts in Washington, D.C. During her career she has been an early childhood classroom teacher, a teacher trainer, and a family therapist. Most recently, Ms. Wasow served as associate dean in the Division of Continuing Education at Bank Street College.

Index

Abbot v. Burke, 45, 51, 156
Aber, J. L., 23, 31
Abington Avenue Elementary School, 78–80, 96–106
Abt Associates, 30
Accelerated Schools approach, 157
Accountability, 40, 42
Active approach to learning, 138
Advocates, 40
African Americans
  approaches to discipline, 121, 131–133
  in Newark school system, 18–19, 37–38, 83, 130
  perspectives of, 145–146, 149–151
  student attitudes toward, 107–108
Agenda-setting dilemma, 11
AIDS, 39, 44
Aid to Families with Dependent Children (AFDC)/Temporary Assistance to Needy Families (TANF), 44
Ajamu, A., 145, 149
ALEM/Community of Learners approach, 157
Ames, L. J., 135, 137
Antler, J., 22
Anyon, Jean, 43, 44, 67, 84, 137
Apple, M., xi
Aronowitz, S., 5–6
Arson, 18, 35, 63
Art, 96–106
Arts High School, 62

Balaban, Nancy, 69, 82–90, 113
Banks, Marva Wright, 124, 125, 126–139

Bank Street College of Education. *See also* Project New Beginnings
  caring approach and, 140–151, 160–167
  developmental-interaction approach and, 21–32, 49–50, 115
  Follow Through program, 21, 22–25, 27–30, 31
  Midtown West (New York City), 153
  overview of public-private partnership, 152–159
  Public School Workshops, 21–27, 31
  Vision 21 Schools (Pittsburgh), 13, 31, 153
Bank Street School for Children, 73, 97
Barnard, Henry, 47
Barringer High School, 36–37, 61, 62
Bennett, Mary, 39
Biber, B., 24, 48
Blachly, Betsy, 69, 71–81, 113
Blizzard, Gladys S., 103, 104
Bojsza, Joan, 69, 91–95
Bolden, Marion, 12, 40, 60–65, 156, 157
Borko, H., 11, 49–50, 114
Bowman, G. W., 28, 30
Bragaw Avenue School, 16, 17
Bredekamp, S., 143
Brown, J. L., 23, 31
Brown Academy, 17
Burke, Lillian, 12, 13–20, 60, 63

Caring, 140–151
  and individual child, 149–151
  in staff development, 140–149, 160–167
Castellano, M., 50

Child-centered approach, 84–90, 98–106, 118–125, 148–149

Children's Literacy Initiative (CLI), 50, 67–68

Clarke, W., 5

Classroom community, 82–90, 120–125

Cleveland School, 34–35

Clinton, Bill, 108, 110

Clinton Avenue Elementary School, 16–18, 63, 75–78, 117–125, 127–135

Coalition of Affordable Housing, 35

Coalition of Essential Schools approach, 157

Cochran-Smith, M., 149

Cohen, D., 113

Collage, 99–100, 104

Collier, M. J., 145–147

Come Look with Me (Blizzard), 103

Comer, J. P., 131–133

Comer approach, 157

Community
 ambivalence toward school reform, 59
 developing classroom, 82–90, 120–125
 involvement of, in schools, 19, 62, 133–135
 in schools, 73

Community Training and Assistance Center (CTAC), 2, 37, 45, 46

Comprehensive School Reform (CSR), 2, 41–42, 50, 51–53

Copple, C., 143

Cotten, Ethel M., 126–139

Counts, George, 48

Cremin, L., 47

Cuban, Larry, xi, 5, 47

Cuffaro, Harriet K., 5, 24, 84, 85–86, 89

Datnow, A., 50

David, J., 111, 113

Delpit, L., 6, 143, 149

Dent, Evangeline, 126–139

Desimore, L., 52

Developmental-interaction approach, 21–32, 49–50, 115

Developmentally appropriate practice, 91–92, 138, 143

Dewey, John, 48, 84–86, 89, 143

Diagnostic Reading Assessment (DRA), 67–68

Direct Instruction, 30

Discipline/classroom management, 121, 126–139
 cultural differences in, xi–xiii, 131–133, 149–150, 164–167
 home versus school approaches to, 131–133

Drug use, 39

DuBois, W. E. B., 146

Edmondson, William, 102

Education Commission of the States, 51–52

Education Resources Group, 31

Ellsworth, J., 135, 137

Elmore, R., 48

Erlichson, B., 51, 52

Experimenting with the World (Cuffaro), 84

Feldman, Richard, 23, 28

Fine, M., 6, 146

Fink, D., 47–48

Fitzgerald, Mary Lee, 37

Florio, Jim, 37

Follow Through program, 21, 22–25, 27–30, 31

Ford Foundation, 156

Fordham, S., 146, 149

Freedom Party, 15

Freire, Paulo, xii, 6

Fullan, Michael, 4, 42, 50, 67

Furman, Lenore, 69, 73, 78–79, 96–106, 113

Gettrell, Merle, 75

Gilkeson, Elizabeth C., 28, 30

Giroux, H., 5–6

Glass, G. V., 30

Goertz, M., 51, 52

Greene, M., 5

Greenfield, P. M., 146

Guided Reading, 67–68

Hale, Janice E., 131–132

Hall, Beverly L., 12, 37–38, 40, 45–46, 54–59, 60, 62, 153–156, 157

Hammond, Margot, 115, 126–139

Hanson, M. J., 146

Hargreaves, A., 50

Harriet Tubman School, 35, 38

Harry, B., 146

Hayes, Kathleen, 69, 96–106, 113
Head Start, 27–28, 73, 91–92, 135–137
Hecht, M. L., 145–147
Heintz, Sandra, 69, 71–81, 113
Henrich, C. C., 23, 31
Herodotus, 158
High-stakes testing, 2, 5, 9–10, 42
Hochwald, E., 9–10, 51
Horton, D., 23
House, E., 30
Hoyle, E., 115
Huron Institute, 30

Identity of students
    African-American teachers and, 18–19,
        140–151
    understanding of, 107–112, 140–141

Jacobs, A., 44
Jenkins, Ella, 71–72
Johnston, R., 46
Jordon, Vernon, 108

Kalyanpur, M., 146
Kappner, Augusta Souza, 115, 152–159
Kennedy, John F., 91
Kindergarten
    high-stakes test and, 2, 9–10
    universal full-day, 55
King, Martin Luther, 75
Kohl, H., 5
Kopacsi, Rosemarie, 9–10, 51, 68, 169–172
Koplow, Lesley, 69, 94, 107–112
Kozol, J., 5

Ladson-Billings, Gloria, ix–xii, 6, 149
Lesch, Judith W., 115, 140–151, 147
Levin, H. M., 5
Lilly, Bob, 34
Lincoln Elementary School, 117, 118
Linn, R. L., 5
Lippman, Carol, 1–7, 12, 13, 33–40, 41–
    53, 60–65, 72, 73, 77
Lipton, M., 42
Little, J., 49
Lucent Technologies, 62
Lynch, E. W., 146

Madden, Nancy, 51
Magnet schools, 34

Mann, Horace, 47
Maple Avenue School, 36–37
Materials, 85–87, 92–93, 99–100, 118–119
Mayer, R., 28
McFarland, Cathy, 12, 33–40, 63
McIntosh, P., 146
McLaughlin, M., 4, 114
McLean, L. D., 30
McNaughton, G., 49
Meetings, classroom, 86–87, 88, 122, 142
Meier, D., 5
Meier, T., 143
Mental health consultants, 94–95, 117–125
Mentoring relationships, 82–90, 93–95,
    96–106
Mercer Avenue School, 140–151
Micklethwait, L., 104
Midtown West (New York City), 153
Miserendino, J., 68, 169
Mitchell, A., 111
Mitchell, Lucy Sprague, 21–22, 24–27,
    48, 113
Montclair Public Schools, 34
Moss, Valerie, 94–95
Music, 71–81
Muslims
    student attitudes toward, 108–109,
        110–111

Nager, N., 24, 48, 115, 149
Nation at Risk, x–xi, 51
New, R. S., 143
Newark, New Jersey. See also Project
    New Beginnings
    arson in, 18, 35, 63
    community involvement in schools,
        19, 62, 133–135
    Comprehensive School Reform (CSR),
        2, 41–42, 50, 51–53
    demographic shifts, x, 35–36, 43–45,
        60–61, 63–64
    in the 1950s, 14
    parent involvement in schools, 19–20,
        38–39, 101–103, 105, 118, 123–
        124, 133–135
    riots of 1967, ix–x, 14–16, 17, 34, 37,
        38, 43–44, 61, 63
    state takeover of schools (1995), 2, 35,
        37–40, 41–42, 45–47, 54–59, 93–
        95, 127, 152–159

Newark Collaboration Group, 36
Newark Economic Development
    Corporation, 36
Newark Museum, 100–104
Newark Teachers' Association, 14, 34–
    35, 38
New Community Corporation, 33–34
New Jersey Core Curriculum Contents
    Standards, 50, 63
New Jersey Department of Education,
    37, 42
New Jersey Education and Law Center,
    51
New Jersey Education Association
    (NJEA), 14, 34
New Jersey Performing Arts Center, 20,
    36, 43
Niemeyer, J. H., 23
Noddings, N., 149

Oakes, J., 42
Office of Early Education, 40
Ogbu, J. U., 146, 149
O'Keefe, Georgia, 103
Onsongo, E., 51, 68
Ounce of Prevention Fund, 162
Our Children and Our Schools
    (Mitchell), 25

Paley, Vivian, 86
Parent involvement in schools, 19–20,
    38–39, 101–103, 105, 118, 123–124,
    133–135
Parents Academies, 39
Parham, T. A., 145, 149
Phillips, C. B., 143
Pizzo, P. D., 136
Poussaint, A. F., 131–133
Powell, L. C., 6, 146
Professional communities
    importance of, 4
Professional development. See Staff
    development
Progressive education, 22, 25, 47–51,
    131, 154, 165
Project New Beginnings, 68. See also
    Newark, New Jersey
    business community and, 155–156
    child-centered approach in, 84–90, 98–
        106, 118–125, 148–149

components of, 62–65, 138–139
described, 1
dilemmas for teachers, 10–11
District/School Leadership Teams, 3,
    10, 58
funding sources, 156–157. See also
    Victoria Foundation
goal of, 42
impact of, 7
implementing, 57–58
integration of disciplines in, 113–115
lessons learned from, 58–59
origins of, 46, 55–59
predecessor programs, 21–32
problems of, 3
as progressive school reform, 48–51
staff development, 55, 67–69, 71–81,
    82–90, 142–143
student outcomes and, 169–172
success of, 3–4
transformation of classrooms, 7, 93–
    95, 148–149
years 3 and 4, 113
years 4 and 5, 114
Prudential Insurance Company, 36, 40, 62
PSE&G, 62
Public School Education Act (1975), 45
Public School Workshops (New York
    City), 21–27, 31
Putnam, R., 11, 49–50, 114

Ravitch, D., 47
Reaves, Mary, 113, 115, 117–125, 126–
    139
Reid, K., 46
Rhine, W. R., 28, 30
Ribeau, S. A., 145–147
Rice, Joseph Meyer, 5
Richardson, George, 15
Richardson, V., 11
Riis, Jacob, 5
Riots of 1967, ix–x, 14–16, 17, 34, 37, 38,
    43–44, 61, 63
Robinson v. Cahill, 45
Roth, Philip, 36

Scheurich, J. J., 146
Schon, D., 167
Schwartz, F., 10, 49–51, 50–51, 68, 115,
    169

Shapiro, A. F., 25
Shapiro, Edna K., 12, 21–32, 24, 48, 115, 149
Shebazz High School, 39
Silin, Jonathan G., 1–7, 10, 12, 41–53, 49–51, 50, 68, 115, 169
Slavin, Robert, 51
Slee, R., 48
Smith, R., 165–166
Smithberg, L. M., 28, 30
Snead, Sandra, 100–101
Source Material Libraries, 26
South Side High School, 63
Staff development, 49–50, 55, 67–69, 114–115
    art in, 96–106
    caring approach in, 140–149, 160–167
    challenges of, 143–145
    child-centered approach and, 142–143, 148–149
    communication and relationships in, 146–148
    creating classroom community, 82–90
    cultural issues in, xi–xiii, 142–143, 150, 164–167
    group approach to, 126–139, 144
    Head Start as model for, 135–137
    importance of, 154
    mentoring relationships in, 82–90, 93–95, 96–106
    music in, 71–81
    trust and, 85, 97
Standards, 14, 16, 42, 50, 63
Stanford Research Institute, 30
Stewart, Jan, 62
Stoll, L., 47–48
Success for All/Roots and Wings, 51, 156, 158

Teacher-centered approach, 97–98, 118, 142–143, 150

Teachers. See also Staff development
    African-American, 18–19, 37–38, 83, 130, 140–151
    empowerment of, 17
    standards for entry-level, 14, 16
13th Avenue School, 36–37
Thompson, A., 148–150
Tomlinson, S., 48
Trust, 85, 97
Turnbull, B., 51
Tyack, David, xi, 5, 47

U.S. Department of Education, 152, 156

Victoria Foundation, 12, 33–40, 46, 57, 60, 63
Vision 21 Schools (Pittsburgh), 13, 31, 153
Vogue Housing, 36

Wagman, Felice, 113, 115, 117–125
Walker, D. F., 30
War on Poverty, 135
Wasley, P., 5
Wasow, Eileen, 115–116, 160–167
Weequahic High School, 36–37
Weiner, G., 48
Weis, L., 6, 146
Werner, E., 165–166
West Side High School, 18–19, 64
White, J. L., 145, 149
Whole-child approach, 24, 91–92
Williams, L. R., 143
Windsor, Charlotte B., 22, 27, 48
Wong, L. M., 6, 146

Yenawine, P., 104
You Can't Say You Can't Play (Paley), 86

Ziebarth, T., 46
Zigler, E. F., 28
Zimiles, H., 28